T0215044

Introducing Bootstrap 4

Create Powerful Web
Applications Using
Bootstrap 4.5

Second Edition

Jörg Krause

Apress®

Introducing Bootstrap 4: Create Powerful Web Applications Using Bootstrap 4.5

Jörg Krause
Berlin, Germany

ISBN-13 (pbk): 978-1-4842-6202-3   ISBN-13 (electronic): 978-1-4842-6203-0
https://doi.org/10.1007/978-1-4842-6203-0

Managing Director, Apress Media LLC: Welmoed Spahr
Acquisitions Editor: Spandana Chatterjee
Development Editor: Rita Fernando
Coordinating Editor: Shrikant Vishwakarma

Cover designed by eStudioCalamar

Cover image designed by Pexels

Distributed to the book trade worldwide by Springer Science+Business Media New York, 233 Spring Street, 6th Floor, New York, NY 10013. Phone 1-800-SPRINGER, fax (201) 348-4505, e-mail orders-ny@springer-sbm.com, or visit www.springeronline.com. Apress Media, LLC is a California LLC and the sole member (owner) is Springer Science + Business Media Finance Inc (SSBM Finance Inc). SSBM Finance Inc is a **Delaware** corporation.

For information on translations, please e-mail booktranslations@springernature.com; for reprint, paperback, or audio rights, please e-mail bookpermissions@springernature.com.

Apress titles may be purchased in bulk for academic, corporate, or promotional use. eBook versions and licenses are also available for most titles. For more information, reference our Print and eBook Bulk Sales web page at http://www.apress.com/bulk-sales.

Any source code or other supplementary material referenced by the author in this book is available to readers on GitHub via the book's product page, located at www.apress.com/978-1-4842-6202-3. For more detailed information, please visit http://www.apress.com/source-code.

Printed on acid-free paper

Table of Contents

About the Author

Jörg Krause has been working with software and software technology since the early 1980s, beginning with a Sinclair and taking his first steps as a programmer in BASIC and assembly language. He studied Information Technology at Humboldt University, Berlin, but left early, in the 1990s, to start his own company. He has worked with Internet technology and software development since the early days when CompuServe and FidoNet dominated. In 1998, he worked on one of the first commercial e-commerce solutions, and wrote his first book in Germany. Due to its wide success, he started working as a freelance consultant and author in order to share his experience and knowledge with others. He has written several books with Apress, Hanser, Addison Wesley, and other major publishers along with several self-published books—a total of over sixty titles. He also publishes articles in magazines and speaks at major conferences in Germany. Currently, Jörg works as an independent consultant, software developer, and author in Berlin. The main focus is web development (nowadays called full-stack), cloud native architectures, and web security. In his occasional spare time, Jörg enjoys reading thrillers and science fiction novels, and playing a round of golf.

About the Technical Reviewer

Kirti Mahadane is a freelance web professional based in India. Since 2015, she has been active in front-end development technologies including Bootstrap. She is particular in writing clean code.

CHAPTER 1

Introduction to Bootstrap

Bootstrap 4.5 is the latest version of the Bootstrap framework, formerly known as Twitter Bootstrap. It was built by Twitter for the mobile-first apps. It's a complete and easy-to-use system of styles that helps deal with the daily tasks of a web developer. Compared with other CSS frameworks, the biggest advantage of Bootstrap is the huge selection of additional templates, themes, and boilerplate code. It makes it very easy and fast to create a sophisticated web site without a design agency or without having any professional design skills. There are also endless additions and extensions available to fill the rare gaps. Moreover, Bootstrap can handle desktop web sites and mobile device pages equally as well, so it's really a one-stop solution.

Where to Obtain Bootstrap

Generally, Bootstrap 4 is distributed using the official web site, `https://getbootstrap.com` and npm (node package manager). Moreover, you also can create your own distribution using the source code. Bootstrap utilizes the raw files of the cascading style sheets language Sass, a pre-compiler that translates into CSS (unlike the previous version, Bootstrap 3, where the primary language was LESS). All common packaging and building tools such as WebPack, SystemJS, or Browserify can be used without restrictions to add Bootstrap directly or from the sources to existing projects.

© Jörg Krause 2020
J. Krause, *Introducing Bootstrap 4*, https://doi.org/10.1007/978-1-4842-6203-0_1

Content Delivery Network

Bootstrap is also available via Bootstrap's own content delivery network (CDN). A CDN enables a web site to frequently retrieve used public files from globally distributed servers. For example, when a user from the United States invokes your host in Germany, the CDN will ensure that the Bootstrap files are retrieved from a server in the United States. This relieves your server, the lines of the provider, and the Internet in general, resulting in a faster download for the user. Basically, this is a win–win situation. If you program on the intranet, a CDN is not to your advantage. If you expect only local users in Germany, there is no advantage to a CDN.

The Bootstrap files are included when using the CDN as follows:

```
1   <link rel="stylesheet"
2         href="https://stackpath.bootstrapcdn.com/
              bootstrap/4.5.0/css/bootstrap.min.css"
3         integrity="sha384-9aIt2nRpC12Uk9gS9baDl411NQApFmC26E
              wAOH8WgZl5MYYxFfc+NcPb1dKGj7Sk"
4         crossorigin="anonymous">
5   <script
6         src="https://stackpath.bootstrapcdn.com/
              bootstrap/4.5.0/js/bootstrap.min.js"
7         integrity="sha384-OgVRvuATP1z7JjHLkuOU7Xw704+h835Lr+
              6QL9UvYjZE3Ipu6Tp75j7Bh/kROJKI"
8         crossorigin="anonymous">
9   </script>
10
11
12  <!--JavaScript support -->
13
14  <script src="https://code.jquery.com/jquery-3.5.1.slim.min.js"
```

```
15        integrity="sha384-DfXdz2htPHOlsSSs5nCTpuj/zy4C+OGp
          amoFVy38MVBnE+IbbVYUew+OrCXaRkfj"
16        crossorigin="anonymous">
17   </script>
18   <script src="https://cdn.jsdelivr.net/npm/popper.
     js@1.16.0/dist/umd/popper.min.js"
19        integrity="sha384-Q6E9RHvbIyZFJoft+2mJbHaEWldlvI9I
          OYy5n3zV9zzTtmI3UksdQRVvoxMfooAo"
20        crossorigin="anonymous">
21   </script>
```

The JavaScript libraries are jQuery for Browser abstraction and DOM access, Popper for notifications, and Bootstrap.js for all the interactive Bootstrap components. If you don't use the components you can remove all three links. If you don't use notification, simply remove Popper. The CSS parts are entirely autonomous and don't need any JavaScript.

Bootstrap 4.5.x   This book was reviewed with version 4.5.0. If you use a newer version, you will need to replace all the version numbers of the type 4.5.0 accordingly.

Repository for Local Installation

To obtain a local copy, you would usually use the node package manager, npm.[1] Npm is both the repository for NodeJs and the tool to access the same. If you develop in Ruby on Rails, you should look for the gem "Bootstrap for Sass."[2] Other environments may come with their own package repositories, but because Bootstrap is entirely for frontend

---

[1]Npm, https://www.npmjs.com.
[2]Gem for Ruby Developers, https://rubygems.org/gems/bootstrap.

development, a package manager from the JavaScript world is the best bet. Here, npm is the most important one. However, the code world is changing constantly and other providers arise all the time, so keep an eye out for new sites for download or public repositories.

Installation Using Npm

Bootstrap can be installed as follows using the npm command line tool:

```
1   $ npm install bootstrap@latest
```

The files are now in the folder *node_modules* of your local project. This gets referenced by whatever development tool you use. Either you add the paths to *index.html* or another start file manually, or let a packer do this. (Packers are beyond the scope of this book, so you need to do your own research.) The example files provided in the Github repository for this book don't use any such dependencies, and use the manual integration instead. This simplifies the setup for beginners.

Bootstrap's file structure in *node_modules/bootstrap* contains three major parts:

- *scss*: Path to Bootstrap's Sass source files

- *js*: Path to Bootstrap's JavaScript source files

- *dist*: Path to Bootstrap's minimized CSS and JS that has been precompiled

Bootstrap was developed in version 4 with Sass.[3] Sass is available on all platforms. Bootstrap uses *Autoprefixer* to work with the vendor prefixes in CSS. If you want to compile Bootstrap by using the Sass source and not use the supplied Gruntfile, you must use an *Autoprefixer* integrated into your own build process. If you use the precompiled Bootstrap files or

---

[3]The Sass Language, http://sass-lang.com.

the Gruntfile, the prefixes are already integrated. The procedure applies to Gulp and other taskRunners equivalent if they are to be used. The appendix reviews this in more depth.

Bootstrap can be downloaded in two types of packages: the compiled version and additionally minimized variants.

Structure of the CSS Files

The complete structure of an environment that uses Bootstrap is as follows:

```
bootstrap/
├── css/
│   ├── bootstrap.css
│   ├── bootstrap.css.map
│   ├── bootstrap.min.css
│   ├── bootstrap.min.css.map
│   ├── bootstrap-grid.css
│   ├── bootstrap-grid.css.map
│   ├── bootstrap-grid.min.css
│   ├── bootstrap-grid.min.css.map
│   ├── bootstrap-reboot.css
│   ├── bootstrap-reboot.css.map
│   ├── bootstrap-reboot.min.css
│   └── bootstrap-reboot.min.css.map
├── js/
│   ├── bootstrap.js
│   ├── bootstrap.min.js
│   ├── bootstrap.js.map
│   ├── bootstrap.min.js.map
│   ├── bootstrap.bundle.js
│   ├── bootstrap.bundle.js.map
│   ├── bootstrap.bundle.min.js
│   └── bootstrap.bundle.min.js.map
```

Precompiled files are the easiest way to use Bootstrap. The *min* versions are additionally minimized (compressed). The *map* files support the developer tools in the browser by mapping the sources to the distributed codes. They are not supposed to be deployed to production environments.

Warning   If you have a Minimizer (sometimes called Minifier or Uglifier) in your project, you pass the nonminimized files (the ones without ".min." infix). Some minimizers destroy the code if it has already been compressed by another minimizer.

In addition to CSS and JavaScript, your app may require fonts that provide the icons. Font symbols are a particularly compact and simple method to incorporate monochrome icons in web sites. Bootstrap 4 does not bundle anything here, and you need to add a font package by yourself. One well- known package is FontAwesome (more on this in Chapter 6, where various icon options are presented). For now, just note that an additional installation step required.

Page-building

Once everything is ready, you can create the first page. This page should provide the basic layout of the entire application. A first version might look like this:

```
1   <!doctype html>
2   <html lang="en">
3     <head>
4       <!-- Required meta tags -->
5       <meta charset="utf-8">
```

```
6      <meta name="viewport" content="width=device-width,
       initial-scale=1, shrink-to-fit=no">

7

8      <!-- Bootstrap CSS -->
9   <link rel="stylesheet" href="https://stackpath.
    bootstrapcdn.com/bootstrap/4.5.0/css/bootstrap.min.css"
    integrity="sha384-9aIt2nRpC12Uk9gS9baDl411NQApFmC26EwAOH8W
    gZl5MYYxFfc+NcPb1dKGj7Sk" crossorigin="anonymous">

10

11

12     <title>Hello, world!</title>
13   </head>
14   <body>
15     <h1>Hello, world!</h1>

16

17     <!-- Optional JavaScript -->
18     <!-- jQuery first, then Popper.js, then Bootstrap JS -->
19   <script src="https://code.jquery.com/jquery-3.5.1.slim.
    min.js" integrity="sha384-DfXdz2htPHOlsSSs5nCTpuj/
    zy4C+OGpamoFVy38MVBnE+IbbVYUew+OrCXaRkfj"
    crossorigin="anonymous"></script>
20   <script src="https://cdn.jsdelivr.net/npm/popper.
    js@1.16.0/dist/umd/popper.min.js" integrity="sha384-Q6E9R
    HvbIyZFJoft+2mJbHaEWldlvI9IOYy5n3zV9zzTtmI3UksdQRVvoxMfoo
    Ao" crossorigin="anonymous"></script>

21

22   </body>
23   </html>
```

The first two metatags from line 5 must be at the beginning of the
block.

Warning   If you load this page locally via *file:///*, consider that some parts may not work as expected. Always try to carry out all stages of development with a local web server (IIS express with Visual Studio, IIS, NodeJs, or a local Apache or nginx are perfect for this).

Note that Bootstrap itself must be loaded after jQuery.

Tip   Download only from a CDN when your web site will be public. For an intranet, a local copy is more suitable.

Browser Support

Even with Bootstrap 4, browser support remains an issue. It has been taken a good deal of effort to reach as many browsers and platforms as it does. Currently it looks like this:

Table 1-1. *Current Browser Support*

	Chrome > 45	Firefox > 38	Edge > 12	Opera > 30	Safari > 9
Android	OK	OK	OK	Not possible	N/A
iOS	OK	N/A	OK	Not possible	OK
MacOS X	OK	OK	OK	OK	OK
Windows	OK	OK	OK	OK	Not possible

Chromium and Chrome for Linux and Firefox for Linux should work, but are not officially supported. The broadest coverage with browsers you currently have is with MacOS and Windows. Internet Explorer is no longer an option in any version, but officially there is support for version 10/11. However, this support will be dropped with Bootstrap 5.

ARIA

Support for barrier-free applications (Accessible Rich Internet Applications Suite = ARIA)[4] is actually an HTML topic. Some examples in the text are already geared and carry these attributes. Here is an overview of how this works. Bootstrap supports ARIA implicitly and comprehensively.

ARIA   Bootstrap's code makes use of several of these ARIA tags and attributes. Even if you don't have any intention of using it, it makes sense to understand something about Bootstrap's internal settings.

HTML5: The Role-Attribute

The role-attribute is set in the relevant HTML tags. It improves semantic markup and thus helps screen readers and other devices to present the correct output. It's part of the effort to help advanced screen readers to render properly and make use of distinct local resources. There is a complete description available online.[5]

For example, imagine a device that has a hardware "search" button. On your page are two forms. One is for searching your site, one for sending a contact form. With `<form role="search">` the device would be able to link the right form to the hardware button, making your page appear a lot more professionally designed.

---

[4]Accessible Rich Internet Applications (WAI-ARIA) 1.1, W3C Recommendation, 14 December 2017, `http://www.w3.org/TR/wai-aria`.

[5]ARIA, "Accessibility and Mozilla," `https://developer.mozilla.org/en-US/docs/Web/Accessibility/ARIA`.

Here is the list of role-attributes:

- banner: The element is a banner

- complementary: The element adds a section, usually instead of an <aside>

- content: Regular content

- info: Additional information

- form: Form

- main: Main area

- navigation: Navigation area

- search: Search

The following role-attributes describe the structure of the page:

- article: Article (text)

- columnheader: Column header

- definition: Definition

- directory: Directory

- document: Document

- group: Group

- heading: Head area

- img: Images

- list: List

- listitem: List item

- math: Mathematical formula

- note: Note, or supplement

- `presentation`: Presentation, display support

- `region`: Area

- `row`: Row

- `rowheader`: Head of a row (left turn)

- `separator`: Separation line in menus or lists

- `toolbar`: Toolbar

An application example looks like this:

```
1    <hr role="separator" />
```

In tags like <nav> or <aside>, the `role`-attribute is redundant. The following is therefore not necessary:

```
1    <nav role="navigation">
2    <aside role="complementary">
```

ARIA Is Not an Issue?   In addition to the barrier-free access, ARIA facilitates semantic attributes that take care and help the maintenance of your pages source code. It is always easier to work with `role="banner"` compared to work interspersed with dozens of `<div>` elements.

Optimization

Correctly created Bootstrap pages can be considerably larger than classic HTML pages. The stability of the styles has its price. You should therefore carefully consider how elements are created. A typical example are long lists with many options. This is where the additions come into the list of elements, buttons, or menus you want to use. This is especially the case when the code is generated on the server. Here's an example:

```
1   <ul class="list-group">
2     <li class="list-group-item">First Element
3     <div class="btn-group">
4       <button type="button"
5               class="btn btn-default dropdown-toggle"
6               data-toggle="dropdown" aria-haspopup="true"
7               aria-expanded="false">
8         Action <span class="caret"></span>
9       </button>
10      <ul class="dropdown-menu">
11        <li><a href="#">Delete</a></li>
12        <li><a href="#">Move</a></li>
13        <li><a href="#">Rename</a></li>
14        <li role="separator" class="divider"></li>
15        <li><a href="#">Download</a></li>
16      </ul>
17    </div>
18    </li>
19    <li>... Other elements</li>
20    <li>... Other elements</li>
21  </ul>
```

This list requires about 530 characters in UTF-16 that are more than 1 KB (in UTF-8 only the characters outside of ASCII have several characters). When you view 40 items on the page, which is not usually a problem because of the drop-downs, there are 40 KB HTML and a payload of roughly 2 KB (40 times the text for each entry with 50 bytes). Here it is worthwhile to use JavaScript.

The following code defines a template with the code of one element, and the JavaScript then adds it to the running time of each list element. For control, HTML5 attributes are used:

```
1   <ul class="list-group" data-list-target>
2     <li class="list-group-item">First Element</li>
3     <li>...other elements</li>
4     <li>...other elements</li>
5   </ul>
6   <div class="btn-group" data-list-template>
7     <button type="button"
8             class="btn btn-default dropdown-toggle"
9             data-toggle="dropdown" aria-haspopup="true"
10            aria-expanded="false">
11      Action <span class="caret"></span>
12    </button>
13      <ul class="dropdown-menu">
14        <li><a href="#">Delete</a></li>
15        <li><a href="#">Move</a></li>
16        <li><a href="#">Rename</a></li>
17        <li role="separator" class="divider"></li>
18        <li><a href="#">Download</a></li>
19      </ul>
20  </div>
```

This is then read by JavaScript using data-list-template attributes to address this portion in the code (line 6), and then cloned at the achievable place through data-list-target attributes. The code block uses jQuery here:

```
1   // Execution if the document was loaded
2   $(function(){
3     // Load Template, clone and hide
4     var template = $('[data-list-template]').hide().clone();
5     // Search list items, Attach copied template, Show
6     $('[data-list-target] li').append($(template).show());
7   });
```

The script will only cost about 250 bytes (130 characters without the comments). Instead of a maximum of 40 KB, this solution requires less than 2.5 KB: if you want it to look more striking, it's 6% of the original size or a decrease of 94%. In addition, the JavaScript code can be outsourced and cached in the browser.

Interactive Surfaces   The script can be further refined so that the switching times only appear when the mouse pointer hovers over the entry. The append is only performed when a mouseenter emerges and mouseleave all buttons are removed. Ensure that events always in some $(document).on('click') pattern, so it works well with the dynamically appended elements. Tip: RTFM jQuery!

Why does this matter for Bootstrap? The smart structure of connected classes and the consequent usage of HTML may lead to many more elements and complex trees compared with pages written entirely manually. It clearly has advantages, and it will speed up your development time. But it will definitely come with a price. And if you want to refine your project, such techniques can be helpful. This is only one example of many such ways to improve performance.

What's New in Bootstrap 4?

This section gives an overview of the changes for those readers switching from Bootstrap 3.

Global Changes

The unit system has been changed from pixels (px) to *rem* (CSS) or *em* (Media Queries). The global font, which serves as the starting point, has been increased from 14 pixels to 16 pixels. This is mainly a reference to higher-resolution screens of mobile devices.

Grid System

So far there have been four raster layers: *xs*, *sm*, *md*, and *lg*. In the future, there will be another level: *xl*. This is designed to support extremely large displays (3,000 x 2,000 pixels and more).

Tables

Tables come with new options:

- *.table-inverse* inverts the table
- *.thead-default* and *.thead-inverse* format the header area
- *.table-sm* creates smaller tables
- All context classes now have the prefix *.table-*
- *.responsive-table* can now be directly assigned to the table element, the container is no longer needed
- *.table-reflow* supports reflow tables

Forms

Instead of the special class *.form-horizontal*, *.row* can now be used. All *.control--* and *.input--*classes were unified to *.form-control-*. This means that the special classes *.has-feedback* and *.help-block* are obsolete.

Buttons

The classes *.btn-default* and *.btn-info* have been omitted in favor of *.btn-secondary*. Another new feature is *.btn-xx-outline*—a bezel button. The class *.btn-xs* is removed.

Pull-Down Menus

Instead of `<ul><li>`-structures, these can now be formatted using `<div><a>`-blocks directly. These are the classes *.dropdown-item* and *.dropdown-menu*. The class *.dropdown-header* can now be applied directly to `<h1>` and the like. Intervals are created with `</div class="dropdown-divider">` rather than the previous method, which used `<li>`-tags.

Panels

The display forms Wells, Panels, and Thumbnails have been deleted and replaced by a new component with the name Card.

Other Updates

Progress bar can now be created with the HTML element `<progress>`. Quotations need the class *.blockquote*. Due to lack of browser support, this has some limitations.

Summary

This chapter covered a short introduction to Bootstrap, ways to obtain it and add it to your web application, and some basics about the internal structure. The major changes from Bootstrap 3 to Bootstrap 4 were explained as well.

CHAPTER 2

It Begins with CSS

Before you begin to use Bootstrap, you should understand the basics of CSS (Cascading Style Sheets). Bootstrap is able to handle most of the obstacles and pitfalls of CSS. This means that a basic knowledge of CSS is enough for a beginner to handle Bootstrap-driven web sites. This chapter will give you a short introduction to CSS. It's not my intention to provide you with in-depth coverage of CSS, as there are many resources available.

CSS is a layout and formatting language for creating and formatting markup languages such as HTML. Ideally, the HTML document contains only semantic information, and with CSS this is then formatted in design and typography.

HTML already provides some basic formatting, such as a larger font for headlines, which can then be customized with CSS. Almost all naturally unformatted elements can be changed in style and appearance by CSS, too. You should not use HTML's formatting attributes to format HTML elements. Most of these attributes and pure formatting elements are obsolete in HTML 5, because the formatting capabilities are replaced by CSS entirely.

With CSS, it is also possible to define output types separately for different devices such as a monitor (screen), projector (projection), and printer (print).

© Jörg Krause 2020
J. Krause, *Introducing Bootstrap 4*, https://doi.org/10.1007/978-1-4842-6203-0_2

Basics

An HTML document consists of semantically meaningful elements for headings, paragraphs, lists, and so forth. The CSS statements must be placed in such a way that the browser can assign styles to these elements.

Basically, there are three ways to store these instructions:

- The `style` attribute that applies to any HTML element, called inline styles.

```
1    <div style="color: green;">Some content</div>
```

- The element `<style></style>`, which summarizes several styles, called internal CSS.

```
1    <style>div { color: green; } </style>
```

- The `<link />` element that references a file that contains multiple style definitions, called external CSS.

```
1    <link rel="stylesheet"
2          type="text/css"
3          href="styles/style.css">
```

The preferred way to store these instructions is to use a separate CSS file. This file can be held in the browser cache and the content can be handled with the appropriate tools so that you can reduce bandwidth (not because of the bandwidth, but because of the associated performance gain). To make a file a CSS file, just add the file extension *.css*.

Local `<style>` elements should be used only in exceptional cases, to temporarily change any complex styles loaded from files. Such local style instructions have a higher priority. The `style`-attribute expands or modifies the styles for a single element only. It has the highest priority over any conflicting rules from the local or imported styles.

Note   Styles form a chain, managed by the priorities mentioned before. You can call it a cascade, too. And that's the reason for the C in CSS: cascading.

The expansion or modification of the style-attribute is the way to let the browser understand how to load the file and treat it as CSS. Note that the path to the file must be specified relative to the HTML document.

Syntax

The syntax of CSS is relatively simple. The basic structure consists of two building blocks:

1. Selector

2. Ruleset

The selector determines for which element or elements the rules apply.

```
1   Selector {
2       Ruleset
3   }
```

When styles are in `style` attributes, they are only valid for that item, and therefore the selector is eliminated.

A ruleset consists of one or many rules. These are to be written in the following form:

```
1   Style: Parameter;
```

The semicolon at the end is mandatory.

Selector

The selector is the instrument that allows the elements on the page to be looked up selectively. The whole scheme of selectors is fairly comprehensive. Here, we'll first cover the most important building blocks.

Elements (Tags)

With CSS, you can address elements' names. The syntax for this is as follows:

```
1    TagName { Ruleset }
```

If you want to change the color of all <p> elements on a page, it is enough to write the following, for example:

```
1    p { color: blue; }
```

IDs

Often, you may want a single tag to be formatted. The tag must be identifiable: that is, it must have an ID (unique identifier for an element) that makes it accessible. The HTML "id" attribute contains a string that is used in the CSS properties. *A unique ID, however, may only be applied to one element within a document and must therefore occur only once.* The syntax for this is as follows:

```
1    #id { }
```

Caution   The ID must not begin with a digit. An underscore is allowed alternatively to any regular letter.

An example of the code for a button looks like this:

```
1   <style>
2   #send {
3     color: red;
4   }
5   </style>
6   <button id="send">Save</button>
```

Classes

Frequently several elements are applied at the same time. To do this we use classes that are written in HTML in the class attribute. You can use multiple classes in the class attribute, divided by spaces, thereby combining rulesets in a smart way. This saves extensive definitions. Bootstrap utilizes this ability comprehensively and is able to achieve complex styling with only a few rulesets. A large number of modification options are available through class combinations. *Unlike IDs, classes may occur more than once in a document.*

The syntax looks like this:

```
1   .class { }
```

An example of two buttons using the same class is shown as follows:

```
1   <style>
2   .btn {
3     color: red;
4   }
5   </style>
6   <button class="btn">Save</button>
7   <button class="btn">Abort</button>
```

Attributes

Attributes can be referenced using the following syntax:

```
1   [name] { }
2   [name="value"] { }
```

An example of another button:

```
1   <style>
2   [data-item] {
3     color: blue;
4   }
5   </style>
6   <button data-item="22">Next</button>
```

If the value of the attribute (to the right of the = sign) is not specified, only the existence of the attribute is considered sufficient to apply the rules. If you specify the value, the quotes must be written, too.

```
1   [data-item="22"] {
2     color: blue;
3   }
```

Logical Selection

It often happens that rulesets are to be applied to multiple selectors. For this purpose, OR logic is required, which is indicated by a comma in CSS:

```
1   a, b { }
```

Between a and b there is no link, so the rule is applied independently to both. The placeholders a and b in the example may be more complex selectors.

Another logical operator is the space (' '). This is a bit odd, as it is hard to read and easy to miss. It applies mostly for classes, where the target element might have multiples. Consider the following two definitions. As similar as they look, they are entirely different:

```
1    .a .b { } .a.b { }
```

Here is a full example:

```
1    <style>
2      .a .b {
3        color: red;
4      }
5      .c.d {
6        color: green;
7      }
8    </style>
9    <div class="a b">
10     A and B
11     <div class="a">A</div>
12     <div class="b">B</div>
13   </div>
14   <div class="c d">C and D</div>
15   <div class="c">C</div>
16   <div class="d">D</div>
```

With the space between the elements, a child element is being addressed. Without, both classes must be used (like an AND operator). In this example, only the div elements "B" (line 12) and "C and D" (line 14) are properly formatted. The class "b" in <div class="a b"> can be omitted—it's useless. If you change the ruleset .c.d into .c,.d (note the comma in the middle), the div elements "C" and "D" become green, too. The reason is that the comma is like an OR operator, so either the first or the second class definition is sufficient to fulfill the rule.

25

More Selectors

In practice, these selectors are not enough. The following table provides a compact overview of all the forms.

Table 2-1. *Simple CSS Selector*

Selector	Description
*	Universal/all
tag	Element
.class	Class (Attribute class)
#id	ID (Attribute id)
[a]	Attribute presence
[a=v]	Attribute value
[a~=v]	Attribute contains a value as a stand-alone word
[a|=v]	Attribute contains no value
[a^=v]	Attribute starts with value
[a$=v]	Attribute ends with value
[a*=v]	Attribute contains a value

Hierarchy Selectors

Dealing with hierarchies is essential to be able to use CSS properly, because HTML documents are hierarchies, which are often called trees. Figure 2-1 shows the relationships between elements in the document tree.

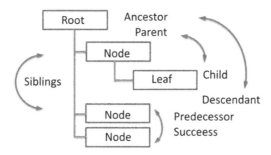

Figure 2-1. *Elements of the hierarchy of a HTML page*

Table 2-2 shows the syntax for CSS.

Table 2-2. *CSS Selectors for Hierarchies*

Selector	Description
|e > f |	Selection if f is a child element of e
|e f |	Selection if f is a descendant of e
|e + f |	Selection if f is a successor of e
|e ~ f |	Selection when e is sibling of f

In contrast to the possibilities of relationships, you might be missing the selectors for the ancestors, predecessors, and parents. You can often achieve this by swapping the elements.

Pseudo Selectors

Pseudo selectors are those that have no comparable representation in HTML, but arise from the position of elements or their use. "Using" an element is primarily user action, such as clicking a hyperlink or placing the cursor in an input field. There are three types of pseudo selectors:

- Static positions (see Table 2-3 for a list of static selectors)

27

Table 2-3. *Static CSS Selectors*

Selector	Description
::first-line	First line
::first-letter	First letter
::before	Before the element
::after	After the element
::selection	The highlighted (selected) area

- Selection of areas (see Table 2-4 for a list of CSS selectors for areas)

Table 2-4. *CSS Selectors for Areas*

Selector	Description
:root	Basic element
:empty	Applies only if the element is empty
:first-child	The first child element of a list
:last-child	The last child element of a list
:nth-child()	A particular child element of a list
:nth-last-child()	A particular child element by the end of a list
:only-child	Valid only when there is only one child element
:first-of-type	First child element of a type
:last-of-type	Last child element of a type
:nth-of-type()	Child element of a type in a list
:nth-last-of-type()	Child element of a type by the end of a list
:only-of-type	Only this type from a list

- Dynamic behavior (see Table 2-5 for a list of dynamic CSS selectors)

Table 2-5. *Dynamic CSS Selectors*

Selector	Description
:link	A hyperlink
:visited	A hyperlink that has already been visited
:hover	A hyperlink with a hovering mouse
:active	A hyperlink that is active (clicked)
:focus	An item that has the focus (blinking cursor)
:target	An item that has a target attribute
:disabled	An item that is disabled (disabled attribute)
:enabled	An item that is enabled (not disabled attribute)
:checked	An item that is checked (only check box)
:valid	An element that is valid
:invalid	An element that is invalid
:lang()	An item that the appropriate lang="" attribute is
:not()	Negates the following selections (this is an operator)

The examination of the validity of form elements presupposes that they were defined in HTML 5 using attributes such as maxlength, required, date, email, and so forth. For the most part, the change of these attributes applies to formatting only. The disabled attribute might be used to let an element appear disabled (grey, less shady, darker), but this might not prevent the element from being clicked. Often you'll need additional JavaScript or change server-side rendering to achieve the intended effect.

Unlike the lang attribute, the function lang() in CSS can determine a fallback to a default culture, that is, responding to the indication of "en-US" on "en" and so on.

Caution   No browser currently sees each of the pseudo-classes shown. The online documentation provides up-to-date information about support that is available at that moment. I recommend visiting W3Schools[1] or Quirksmode[2] for more information.

Units

CSS units express length specifications. This is needed for widths, heights, spacing, margins, and so forth. Unit information consists syntactically from a number and a unit. For the number 0 the unit can be omitted. There are two types of units: absolute and relative.

Absolute Units

Absolute units are as follows:

- cm: Centimeters

- mm: Millimeters

- in: Inches

- px: Pixels

---

[1]W3Schools, "CSS Browser Support Reference," http://www.w3schools.com/cssref/css3_browsersupport.asp.

[2]Quirksmode, "CSS Contents and Browser Compatibility," http://www.quirksmode.org/css/contents.html.

- pt: Points

- pc: Picas

Caution   Typographic units such as points and picas are holdovers from the era of paper printing. There you could define the exact widths when printing: 1 pica is 12 points, 1 point is 1/72 of an inch. In today's world of screens with many sizes, widths and resolutions such information is largely pointless.

The relationship between pixel (screen dot) and physical space is set at Microsoft Windows as 1 inch = 2.54 cm = 96 pixels. Standard devices with standard definition deliver a ratio of 1 device pixel = 1 pixel. High resolution devices, such as printers or retina displays, provide n = 1 device pixel pixels. Table 2-6 gives some additional details:

Table 2-6. *Media Query in the HTML Document*

System	Resolution (pixels per inch)	Device pixels per pixel
Mac	72	1
Windows	96	1
Mobil low	120	1
Mobil medium	160	2
Mobil high	240	2
Retina	300	3

If you wish to find out the real resolution, you can only do this by specifying the screen width and height and the size of the screen. At 4.65 inches (for a Smartphone) and 1,280 x 720 pixels, this is given by the Pythagorean theorem:

```
1    sqrt(1280² x 720²) / 4.65 = 315.8
```

This is rounded up to 316 and generally marketed as 320 dpi. Divided by 96 gives a ratio of 1:3.33, which is rounded as 3 device pixels per virtual pixel.

Generally, absolute data should be used only if the output can be determined with certainty. This is possible only in the case of printers.

Tip   If you need an absolute unit, you should resort to *px* when you use a screen. On a printer, you should mostly use *mm* or *pt*.

Relative Units

Relative units use a specific starting point, because they calculate only ratios. Available are the following units:

- em: Unit of font size, based on the height in pixels (1 em is the size in pixels of the base font's uppercase letter "M")

- ex: Unit of font size, based on the height of the lowercase letter "x"

- ch: Unit of font size, based on the width of the digit "0"

- rem: Unit of font size, based on the width of the lowercase letter "m" of the root element of the page (body)

- vw: Relative to 1% of the width of the viewport (46 cm screen width is 1 vw = 0.46 cm)

- vh: Relative to 1% of the height of the viewport

- vmin: Relative to 1% of the width of the narrow side of the viewport

- vmax: Relative to 1% of the width of the wide side of the viewport

- %: Percentage to the original value

The unit *em* used in typography defines the size of the uppercase letter "M" as a measure of unity. This is not the case with CSS, where the value is comparable with the browser default font Times New Roman. Which concrete pixel value the browser uses is not clearly defined. The concrete pixel value is not 12 pixels as is often claimed, and even the more frequently encountered 16 pixels is not a guarantee.

Figure 2-2 shows the default font for Firefox. It uses 16 pixels for the letter "M," which is equivalent to specifying 16px. The underline is 16 pixels wide. As font size was adjusted to 1 em or 16px at this screenshot, the achieved result is the same. That's one of the reasons the Bootstrap framework defines an entry point for all font sizes as 16px. It ensures what would be otherwise just an assumption.

Figure 2-2. *Measurement of the pixels of the em unit*

Tip   If you need a relative unit, you should use *em* or *rem*. The unit *rem* has the advantage in that it stays constant over the entire page, whereas *em* applies to the most current font.

The Box Model

HTML has two types of forms of representation for elements: flow and block. Flow elements embed themselves in the running text. These elements have dimensions such as width and height, for they depend on the surrounded content. On the other hand, block element dimensions cause adjacent elements to be displaced from their occupied space, and they can define the width and height they occupy by themselves. Moreover, the displacement behavior is highly customizable, up to the desired superposition. With special rules, elements that are actually floating elements are misidentified as block elements. This also can be reversed.

Figure 2-3 shows an example of a box model with the defined properties of the block elements for almost all rectangular areas.

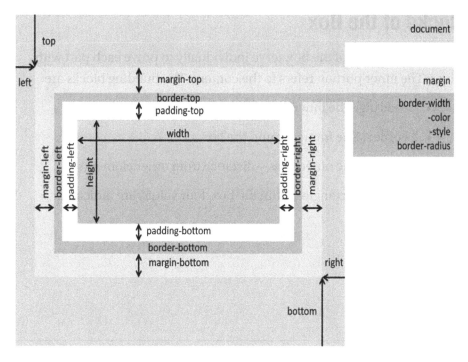

Figure 2-3. *Blocks of the box-models*

It is important to realize that the indication of the width and height are not the final dimensions, but the dimensions of the content area mapped. When a frame is enclosing the box with equal frame width on all sides, the frame width needs to be charged twice for the calculation of the final width, which makes the box dimensions on all sides equal to:

1   Width = Margin * 2 + Border width * 2 + Padding * 2
2   Height = Margin * 2 + Border width * 2 + Padding * 2

As there are differences between the paddings, border widths, and spacings, the calculation is accordingly complex. What's graphically called a frame here is technically assigned as a "border," assuming that the four sides are usually not exactly the same.

Blocks of the Box

The building blocks of the box serve individually to prove each part with values. The inner portion refers to the content. The building blocks are:

- `padding`: The inner distance from content to border
- `border`: The frame around the box
- `margin`: The outer edge—distance from other elements

Because it is a rectangle within the box, four values are indicated:

- `top`
- `right`
- `bottom`
- `left`

Counting   The coordinate origin begins at the top left of your screen or printed page. Some rules can be equal to specify multiple values. In such cases, the four values are interpreted in the order shown, starting with the top (upper left) and then continuing clockwise.

The `margin` that formed the horizontal distances is absolutely valid. The vertical distance, in contrast, may under certain circumstances coincide (collapse). This occurs when no frame (`border`) or spacing (`padding`) is used and no exemption (`clear`) takes place. Here the lower edge of the upper box is overlaid with the upper edge of the lower box. If there are edges of different size, the wider edge is taken as the whole edge.

Exceptions   There are a number of exceptions from the reunification rules of the edges. For more information, especially for complex pages, consult the official documentation on W3C Org's CSS page.[3]

Box Model Extensions

An extension of the CSS box model introduced in CSS 3 allows even more flexibility in allocation. It provides a more fine-grained setting for the behavior of a box (which are, in fact, just rectangular areas on the page). Using the box-sizing property lets you specify to which extent details are available from width or height. Allowed values are one of the following:

- content-box: Data is only valid for the content. This is the default behavior.

- padding-box: Information applies to the content and padding.

- border-box: Information applies to content, padding, and frame.

- inherit: Inherits the setting of its parent element.

This example shows how to use the rule:

```
1   #content-box {
2       box-sizing: content-box;
3   }
4   #border-box {
5       box-sizing: border-box;
6   }
```

---

[3]W3C, "What Is CSS?," https://www.w3.org/Style/CSS.

The Flexbox Model

The flexbox model (also known as the flexible box model, flexbox layout, or "flex layout") was introduced to solve the challenge of aligning elements and distributing space in a container. The size of the available space is usually unknown or dynamic. The flexbox model gives great control for almost all possible layout options.

The properties supported by the flexbox model allow the modification of an item's width, height, and order. We can define the behavior to use the available space even if the user changes the browser dimensions. Items can be shrinked and expanded to fill the space perfectly.

A layout based on flexbox model instructions is direction-agnostic. You can arrange the items based on different rules that apply if the available space changes or the application resizes.

Tip   Compared to the grid model layout, explained in the next section, the flexbox model provides better support for components based applications, were only few visible elements compete for space.

Terminology

The flexbox model uses terms that are relatively new to CSS:

- Container: A container is the space where the items are being arranged

- Items: An item is a single element that takes space in the container

Both are controlled by a set of properties that CSS can apply. The actual element in HTML is not that important. While almost all examples use <div> elements, it is not limited to that.

Container

To create a container you use an element and apply this rule:

```
1   .container {
2     display: flex; /* or inline-flex */
3   }
```

Naming the class *container* has no meaning apart from documentation. Be aware that some frameworks may use the same technique inside and may also use such as class name.

Once we have a container it's time to control the order of the items. This is what `flex-direction` is for:

```
1   .container {
2     flex-direction: row | row-reverse | column |
      column-reverse;
3   }
```

This establishes the main axis, thus defining the direction the items are placed in the container. Flexbox is (aside from optional wrapping) a *single-direction layout* concept. Think of flex items as primarily laying out either in horizontal rows or vertical columns. Here are the options:

- `row` (default): left to right in ltr; right to left in rtl
- `row-reverse`: right to left in ltr; left to right in rtl
- `column`: same as row but top to bottom
- `column-reverse`: same as row-reverse but bottom to top

However, the space for one row is usually very limited. The items will therefore need to wrap to the next line. That's why the property flex-wrap exists. It changes the behavior if the items do not fit on one line.

```
1   .container {
2     flex-wrap: nowrap | wrap | wrap-reverse;
3   }
```

- nowrap (default): all flex items will be on one line

- wrap: flex items will wrap onto multiple lines, from top to bottom

- wrap-reverse: flex items will wrap onto multiple lines from bottom to top

The additional property flex-flow applied to the container is a shorthand for the flex-direction and flex-wrap properties, which together define the flex container's main and cross axes. The default value is row nowrap.

```
1   flex-flow: <'flex-direction'> || <'flex-wrap'>
```

The justify-content flex items within a flex container demonstrates the different spacing options. It tries to distribute the space between items equally, if the items cannot resize itself due to content or other restrictions, such as reaching their maximum width. IT can also be an option to control the behavior if an overflow happens at the end of the line.

```
1   .container {
2     justify-content: flex-start | flex-end | center |
      space-between | space-around | space-evenly | start | end
      | left | right ... + safe | unsafe;
3   }
```

- `flex-start` (default): items are laid out to the start of the `flex-direction`.

- `flex-end`: items are laid out to the end of the `flex-direction`.

- `start`: items are laid out to the start of the `writing-mode` direction.

- `end`: items are laid out to the end of the `writing-mode` direction.

- `left`: items are laid out to left edge of the container, unless that doesn't make sense with the `flex-direction`, then it behaves like start.

- `right`: items are laid out to right edge of the container, unless that doesn't make sense with the `flex-direction`, then it behaves like start.

- `center`: items are centered along the line.

- `space-between`: items are evenly distributed in the line; first item is on the start line, last item on the end line.

- `space-around`: items are evenly distributed in the line with equal space around them. Visually the spaces aren't necessarily equal, since all the items have equal space on both sides. The first and last item doesn't have a predecessor or successort, hence the space is only one of the given units.

- `space-evenly`: items are distributed so that the spacing between any two items (and the space at start and end) is equal.

You can also pair these values with two other keywords: `safe` and `unsafe`. Safe means here that you can't render items in a way that they are off-screen to either side and would be no longer visible.

More alignment options are provided by `align-items`. The alignment applies against the parent's top or bottom, or along a baseline. Hence it applies to the vertical distribution of items.

```
1   .container {
2     align-items: stretch | flex-start | flex-end | center |
      baseline | first baseline | last baseline | start | end |
      self-start | self-end + ... safe | unsafe;
3   }
```

- `stretch` (default): stretch to fill the container (this will respect min-width/max-width).

- `flex-start` / `start` / `self-start`: items are placed at the start of the cross axis. The difference between these three keywords is subtle, and has to do with respecting the flex-direction rules or the writing-mode rules.

- `flex-end` / `end` / `self-end`: items are placed at the end of the cross axis. The difference again is subtle and is about respecting flex-direction rules versus writing-mode rules.

- `center`: items are centered in the cross axis.

- `baseline`: items are aligned such as their baselines align.

Again, the `safe` and `unsafe` modifier keywords prevent content from being rendered invisible or not.

A similar option is `align-content`, which is used to group items in a cluster. The whole cluster can be at the top or bottom, or stretch out to fill the space, or have equal spaces between the items. This aligns a flex container's lines within when there is extra space in the cross axis, similar to how justify-content aligns individual items within the main axis. If there is only one line of flex items this property has no meaning:

```
1   .container {
2     align-content: flex-start | flex-end | center |
      space-between | space-around | space-evenly | stretch |
      start | end | baseline | first baseline | last baseline +
      ... safe | unsafe;
3   }
```

- flex-start / start: items are laid out according to the start of the container. flex-start honors the flex-direction while start honors the writing-mode direction.

- flex-end / end: items laid out to the end of the container. The (more support) flex-end honors the flex-direction while end honors the writing-mode direction.

- center: items are centered in the container.

- space-between: items are evenly distributed; the first line is at the start of the container while the last one is at the end.

- space-around: items are evenly distributed with equal space around each line.

- space-evenly: items are evenly distributed with equal space around them.

- stretch (default): lines stretch to take up the remaining space.

The safe and unsafe modifier keywords can be used here as well.

Items

Items are usually laid out by the containers options. In some cases it might be necessary to align single items differently. The few options CSS provides here are described as follows.

You can change the order. By default, flex items are laid out in the source order (as they appear in HTML). However, the order property controls a different order in which they appear in the flex container.

```
1   .item {
2     order: <integer>; /* default is 0 */
3   }
```

The rule flex-grow allows an item to grow if the items' size is not equal. It gives the ability for a flex item to grow if necessary. It accepts a unitless value that serves as a proportion. It dictates what amount of the available space inside the flex container the item should take up. If all items have flex-grow set to 1, the remaining space in the container will be distributed equally to all children. If one of the children has a value of 2, the remaining space would take up twice as much space as the others (or it will try to).

```
1   .item {
2     flex-grow: <number>; /* default 0 */
3   }
```

The rule flex-shrink also defines the ability for a flex item to shrink if necessary.

```
1   .item {
2     flex-shrink: <number>; /* default 1 */
3   }
```

The rule `flex-basis` defines the default size of an element before the remaining space is distributed. It can be a length (e.g., 20%, 5rem) or a keyword. The `auto` keyword means "look at my width or height property."

```
1   .item {
2     flex-basis: <length> | auto; /* default auto */
3   }
```

If `flex-basis` is set to 0; the extra space around content isn't factored in. If set to auto, the extra space is distributed based on its flex-grow value.

The shorthand rule `flex` combines the rules for `flex-grow`, `flex-shrink`, and `flex-basis` combined. The second and third parameters (`flex-shrink` and `flex-basis`) are optional. The default is 0 1 auto, but if you set it with a single number value, then it is like <number> 1 0.

```
1   .item {
2     flex: none | [ <'flex-grow'> <'flex-shrink'>? ||
      <'flex-basis'> ]
3   }
```

The shorthand sets the other values intelligently. That makes it more robust and easier to use.

The Grid Model

The grid model layout is the most powerful way to arrange items on the screen using pure CSS. It creates a two-dimensional system, using rows and columns. The flexbox model described earlier is more of a one-dimensional layout, with a single line that breaks at well-defined borders. In a two-dimensional layout you need to define a container (the grid container) and the containers items (grid items).

You can think of the grid model as an extremely powerful and flexible way to create tables.

Terminology

Some terms help to understand the explanations that follow. These terms are new to CSS and came with the grid model.

- Grid container: Made with the `display: grid` rule. It is the direct parent of all the grid items.

- Grid item: The children (i.e., direct descendants) of the grid container.

- Grid line: The dividing lines that make up the structure of the grid. They can be either vertical ("column grid lines") or horizontal ("row grid lines") and appear on either side of a row or column.

- Grid track: The space between two adjacent grid lines. You can think of them like the columns or rows of the grid, that's the space where the items reside.

- Grid cell: The space between two adjacent rows and two adjacent column grid lines. Think of it as just a virtual space for an item.

- Grid area: The total space surrounded by four grid lines. A grid area may be composed of any number of grid cells. It is like merging cells into a larger space.

Grid Container Properties

The rule `display` defines the element as a grid container and establishes a new grid formatting context for its contents by applying one of these values:

- `grid`: generates a block-level grid

- `inline-grid`: generates an inline-level grid

```
1    .container {
2      display: grid | inline-grid;
3    }
```

The rules `grid-template-columns` and `grid-template-rows` define the columns and rows of the grid with a list of values, divided by spaces. The values represent the track size, and the space between them represents the grid line. The values for track-size can be a length, a percentage, or a fraction of the free space in the grid. `line-name` is an arbitrary name of your choosing. Fractions use the special unit fr. This is a number only, giving the number of parts an item can cover, depending on the number of items. If you have four items and a 1fr, the item covers one of the fractions. For four items these are four, hence it's the same as 25%. However, if a fifth item appears, the 1fr would drop to 20%. This makes it very flexible, more so than the percentage value.

```
1    .container {
2      grid-template-columns:  ... |   ...;
3      grid-template-rows:  ... |   ...;
4    }
```

The number of arguments depends on the number of columns or rows, respectively:

```
1    .container {
2      grid-template-columns: 40px 50px auto 50px 40px;
3      grid-template-rows: 25% 100px auto;
4    }
```

You can choose to explicitly name the lines. Note the bracket syntax for the line names:

```
1   .container {
2     grid-template-columns: [first] 40px [linetwo] 50px
      [linethree] auto [colfourstart] 50px [five] 40px [end];
3     grid-template-rows: [rowonestart] 25% [rowoneend] 100px
      [third] auto [lastrow];
4   }
```

That leads to a grid with user named lines. A line can have more than one name. For example, here the second line will have two names: rowoneend and rowtwostart:

```
1   .container {
2     grid-template-rows: [rowonestart] 25% [rowoneend
      rowtwostart] 25% [rowtwoend];
3   }
```

If your definition contains repeating parts, you can use the repeat() notation to shorten your code:

```
1   .container {
2     grid-template-columns: repeat(3, 20px [col-start]);
3   }
```

This is a shorthand equivalent to the following definition:

```
1   .container {
2     grid-template-columns: 20px [col-start] 20px [col-start]
      20px [col-start];
3   }
```

If multiple lines share the same name, they can be referenced by their line name and count.

```
1   .item {
2     grid-column-start: col-start 2;
3   }
```

The fr unit allows you to set the size of a track as a fraction of the free space of the grid container, as shown in the next example:

```
1   .container {
2     grid-template-columns: 1fr 1fr 1fr;
3   }
```

The free space is calculated after any nonflexible items. In this example the total amount of free space available to the *fr* units doesn't include the fixed *50 px* value:

```
1   .container {
2     grid-template-columns: 1fr 50px 1fr 1fr;
3   }
```

The property grid-template-areas defines a template by referencing the names of the grid areas created with the grid-area property. Repeating the name of a grid area causes the content to span (merge) those cells. A period signifies an empty cell. The value *grid-area-name>* is the name of a grid area specified with grid-area. A period signifies an empty grid cell and the value *none* defines that there are no grid areas at all:

```
1   .container {
2     grid-template-areas:
3       " | . | none | ..."
4       "...";
5   }
```

A more complex example follows:

```
1   .item-a {
2     grid-area: header;
3   }
4   .item-b {
5     grid-area: main;
6   }
7   .item-c {
8     grid-area: sidebar;
9   }
10  .item-d {
11    grid-area: footer;
12  }
13
14  .container {
15    display: grid;
16    grid-template-columns: 50px 50px 50px 50px;
17    grid-template-rows: auto;
18    grid-template-areas:
19      "header header header header"
20      "main main . sidebar"
21      "footer footer footer footer";
22  }
```

This will create a grid that is four columns wide by three rows tall. The top row will be composed of the header area only. The middle row will be composed of two main areas, one empty cell, and one sidebar area. The bottom row is all footer.

The property `grid-template` is a shorthand for setting `grid-template-rows`, `grid-template-columns`, and `grid-template-areas` in one step.

Spaces between columns and rows are defined by column-gap and row-gap. Gaps set the width of the gutters between the columns or rows. The values are standard length units.

```
1   .container {
2     grid-template-columns: 100px 50px 100px;
3     grid-template-rows: 80px auto 80px;
4     column-gap: 10px;
5     row-gap: 15px;
6   }
```

According the other rules a property grid-gap exists, which is a shorthand for row-gap and column-gap properties.

Handling Items in the Grid

The property justify-items aligns grid items along the inline (row) axis. Compare this to align-items that aligns along the column axis. This value applies to all items inside the container.

```
1   .container {
2     justify-items: start | end | center | stretch;
3   }
```

Here are the possible values with short explanations:

- start: aligns items to justify with the start edge of their cell

- end: aligns items to justify with the end edge of their cell

- center: aligns items in the center of their cell

- stretch: fills the whole width of the cell (default)

The property is accompanied by `align-items`, which aligns items along the column axis. This value applies to all grid items inside the container.

- `start`: aligns items to justify with the start edge of their cell

- `end`: aligns items to justify with the end edge of their cell

- `center`: aligns items in the center of their cell

- `stretch`: fills the whole height of the cell (default)

```
1   .container {
2     align-items: start | end | center | stretch;
3   }
```

This behavior can also be set on individual grid items using the `align-self` property. A `place-items` property exists to combine both, the `align-items` and `justify-items` properties in a single declaration as a shorthand.

The total size of your grid might be less than the size of its grid container. Using items with nonflexible units such as *px* can cause this behavior. In this case you can set the alignment of the whole grid within the grid's container. That's where the property `justify-content` comes into play. This property aligns the grid along the row axis. Accordingly the, `align-content` property aligns the grid along the column axis. Here are the available values:

- `start`: aligns the grid to be justified with the start edge of the grid container

- `end`: aligns the grid to be justified with the end edge of the grid container

- `center`: aligns the grid in the center of the grid container

- `stretch`: resizes the grid items to allow the grid to fill the full width of the grid container

- space-around: places an even amount of space between each item, with half-sized spaces on the far ends

- space-between: places an even amount of space between each item, with no space at the far ends

- space-evenly: places an even amount of space between each item, including the far ends

```
1   .container {
2       justify-content: start | end | center | stretch |
            space-around | space-between | space-evenly;
3   }
```

Same relation happens between content and grid. Here you use align-content.

```
1   .container {
2       align-content: start | end | center | stretch |
            space-around | space-between | space-evenly;
3   }
```

Implicit Tracks

The properties grid-auto-columns, grid-auto-rows specify the size of any auto-generated grid tracks, often called implicit grid tracks. Implicit tracks are created when there are more grid items than cells or when a grid item is placed outside of the explicit grid. The unit is a length unit.

```
1   .container {
2       grid-template-columns: 60px 60px;
3       grid-template-rows: 90px 90px;
4   }
```

This creates a 2 x 2 grid.

Automatic Parts

If you have grid items that you don't explicitly place on the grid, the auto-placement algorithm places the items for you. The auto properties controls how the algorithm works. Use `grid-auto-columns, grid-auto-rows,` and `grid-auto-flow` with these values, respectively:

- `row`: fill in each row by adding new rows as necessary (default)

- `column`: fill in each column by adding new columns as necessary

- `dense`: fill in holes earlier in the grid if smaller items come up later

```
1   .container {
2     grid-auto-flow: row | column | row dense | column
      dense;
3   }
```

Caution   `dense` changes only the visual order of your items and might cause them to appear out of order. That could raise issues with accessibility.

Grid Item Properties

The properties for the children, called grid items, provide a more fine-grained control, using these properties:

- `grid-column-start`
- `grid-column-end`

- grid-row-start
- grid-row-end

These properties determine a grid item's location within the grid by referring to specific grid lines. The allowed values are the following:

- <line>: can be a number to refer to a numbered grid line, or a name to refer to a named grid line

- span <number>: the item will span across the provided number of grid tracks (merge cells)

- span <name>: the item will span across until it hits the next line with the provided name (merge cells)

- auto: indicates auto-placement, an automatic span, or a default span of one

```
1   .item {
2     grid-column-start:  |  | span  | span  | auto;
3     grid-column-end:  |  | span  | span  | auto;
4     grid-row-start:  |  | span  | span  | auto;
5     grid-row-end:  |  | span  | span  | auto;
6   }
```

If no grid-column-end or grid-row-end is given, the item will span one track by default. Items can overlap if the placement enforces this. You can use the z-index rule to control their stacking order.

Compliance with Media

With CSS you may set the presentation of a document for different output media. Media queries are used to assign a style sheet to a medium. It's called "query" because the output device is being asked for its type and capabilities in order to apply rules properly.

A media query list for criteria must meet an output medium so that a style sheet is included for processing. Media queries consist of a media type (e.g., screen or printer), a media characteristic (such as color capability), or a combination of both. By using the possibility of a combination, you can tailor a variety of output media style sheets.

Caution   Media queries cannot be quoted in `style`-attributes. You must use CSS files referenced using a `<link />` element.

Syntax

Specifying a media type is a simple keyword, for example, `screen`.

Tip   If no media query is specified or the specified query consists only of spaces, the default is `all`. The following shows a media query in a HTML document.

```
1    <link rel="stylesheet" href="monitor.css" media="screen">
2    <link rel="stylesheet" href="printer.css" media="print">
```

The `print` media type ensures that the style sheet *printer.css* is used only when printing. On the other hand, on a screen (`screen`) *monitor.css* is activated.

Caution   This procedure has the disadvantage that both style sheets often contain the same CSS rules. In addition, at least two files are needed.

You can also omit the attribute media; then the style sheet in question applies to all media. Then the only changes need to be stated in the alternative file.

```
1   <link rel="stylesheet" href="monitor.css">
2   <link rel="stylesheet" href="printer.css" media="print">
```

Alternatively, the rules can be accommodated directly in the CSS file.

```
1   @media print {
2     /* Rules for printing */
3   }
```

Media have certain characteristics that modify the selection rule. With a screen this can be the number of pixels, for example. Prefixes such as min- and max- allow you to specify areas.

```
1   <link rel="stylesheet" href="pt.css"
2         media="(orientation: portrait)">
```

The style sheet *pt.css* is included if the contents of web pages in portrait orientation (portrait) are issued.

```
1   <style type="text/css" media="(color)">
2     /* color rules written here */
3   </style>
```

The color properties specified in the style element are processed when the output medium is set to reproduce colors. A black-and-white printer would then benefit from not having any nonreadable colors on output (e.g., yellow on white).

```
1   @import 'layout.css' (min-width: 150mm);
```

The style sheet *layout.css* will apply when the display area of the output medium is at least 150 mm.

Media queries can be grouped with a logical OR. The comma is used the same as it is with the CSS selectors. Grouped queries are completely independent. Apply one of the queries at least when the declarations are applied.

```
1   @media print, embossed {
2       /* Formats for print media. */
3   }
```

In this example, a style sheet is specified, which can be used both for print media type and the embossed media type.

Several media features may be associated with the and operator. A style sheet will only be processed if all of the membership criteria are met.

```
1   @media (min-width: 130mm) and (max-width: 160mm) {
2       /* compact Layout */
3   }
4   @media print and (color), screen and (color) {
5       /* color */
6   }
```

The media type listed at the beginning of a media query (as in this note) can contain the keywords only or not. only hides the media query to browsers that do not support this and related combinations. Otherwise, the query is processed as if the keyword was not there. If a media query operator not is used the query is denied (negated).

```
1   @media only all and (min-width: 150mm) {
2       /* Layout */
3   }
4   @media not all and (monochrome) {
5       /* color */
6   }
```

This example shows how screens are assigned to a minimum 150 mm wide display area rules. A browser that understands media queries is ignoring the keyword only. By denying the query *monochrome*, the media that can deal with color can be utilized.

Dealing with Units   A special concern is one related to lengths units *em* or *ex*. In the processing of these values the default of the browser is assumed, which has been defined by the user (or his operating system). Normally *em* refers to the current font, which has not yet been defined at the level of the media query. More explanations about units can be found at the end of this chapter.

Each feature can also be used without a value. In this case, it is determined whether the feature is present on the medium used.

```
1   @media (width) {
2      /* The output medium has the characteristic "width" */
3   }
4   @media (color) {
5      /* The output medium has the characteristic "color
          capability"  */
6   }
```

Parameters

The feature width is described in continuous media as the width of the display area (viewport) and paged media as the width of a page. The prefixes *min-* and *max-* are allowed to specify limits.

```
1   @media (width: 60em) {
2      /* width corresponds exactly 60em  */
3   }
```

```
4   @media (min-width: 50em) {
5     /* width is at least  50em */
6   }
7   @media (max-width: 70em) {
8     /* width shall not exceed 70em */
9   }
```

Tip   If you use features that relate to the display area, it is almost always a good idea to use one of the possible prefixes. The actual display width the user has cannot always be reliably predicted.

The feature height describes, in continuous media, the height of the display area (viewport) and paged media as the height of a page. The prefixes *min-* and *max-* are allowed to specify limits.

The features device-width (device's width) and device-height (device's height) describe the width or height of the output device (e.g., the width of the screen in pixels). The value is a positive length specification. The prefixes *min-* and *max-* are allowed to specify limits.

```
1   @media (device-width: 800px) {
2     /* width corresponds exactly to 800 Pixel */
3   }
4   @media (min-device-width: 800px) {
5     /* width is at least 800px */
6   }
7   @media (max-device-width: 1024px) {
8     /* width is not more than 1024px */
9   }
```

Caution   Even if an output device has certain dimensions, it says nothing about whether the available range is also used. Also, the measure of the pixels differ from the physical pixels—for example, this may be the case with retina displays. Likewise, for all devices that do not report their orientation, the value may not change. For Apple, the width stays the same in portrait mode—even if the user rotates the device and uses it in landscape format. Thus, you must be aware of orientation and test carefully.

The feature orientation describes the page format of an output medium. The orientation corresponds to the value landscape (horizontal), when the value of the feature width is greater than the value of the feature height. Otherwise, the orientation corresponding to the value portrait (vertical). The value is one of either portrait or landscape.

```
1    @media (orientation: portrait) {
2      /* formats for portrait format output media */
3    }
```

The characteristic aspect-ratio (aspect ratio) is the ratio of the feature width to feature height. The value is a ratio value. The prefixes *min-* and *max-* are allowed here.

```
1    @media (aspect-ratio: 4/3) { /* Fall 1 */ }
2    @media (min-aspect-ratio: 4/3) { /* Fall 2 */ }
3    @media (max-aspect-ratio: 4/3) { /* Fall 3 */ }
```

In this example, the ratio value is assigned to the 4/3 variants of aspect-ratio-feature. The style sheet is processed if the aspect ratio of the display area (viewport) is exactly 4 to 3 equivalent (case 1). That is the case for example with a display area of 492 to 369 pixels. The style sheet in case 2 is applied if the aspect ratio is 4/3 or greater (e.g., 5/3 or 6/3).

In case 3, the style sheet is processed accordingly only when the aspect ratio is 4/3 or less (for example, 2/3 or 1/3).

The feature device-aspect-ratio (the device's aspect ratio) describes the ratio of the characteristic device-width to feature device-height. The application is similar to the feature aspect-ratio.

The feature color describes the number of bits that a device for each color component (that is, red, green or blue) can use. If the output device display these colors, the value 0 (zero) is true. If different color components use different numbers of bits, then count the lowest bit number the device uses. The value is a non-negative number.

```
1   @media (color: 2) { /* Simple color layout */ }
2   @media (min-color: 3) { /* Complex color layout */ }
3   @media (max-color: 2) { /* Simple color layout */ }
```

The characteristic color-index describes the number of color definitions in the color table of the output medium. If the media does not have a color table, the value 0 (zero) is true. Usually, the media only has a color chart where the color capability is limited.

```
1   @media (color-index: 16) {
2     /* exactly 16 colors available */
3   }
4   @media (min-color-index: 20) {
5     /* At least 20 colors are available */
6   }
7   @media (max-color-index: 256) {
8     /* more than 256 colors are available */
9   }
```

Caution   Support for color-index is currently deficient in all browsers.

The feature monochrome (black and white) describes the number of bits that are used to describe a black-white hue. If it is not a device that can only display grayscale (also colors), the value 0 (zero) is true.

```
1    @media (monochrome: 1) {
2        /* only black and white are available */
3    }
4    @media (min-monochrome: 4) {
5        /* At least 16 gray levels are available */
6    }
7    @media (max-monochrome: 8) {
8        /* more than 256 gray levels are available */
9    }
```

The characteristic light-level (brightness) describes the ambient lighting conditions, which are detected by the brightness sensor of the camera. The following settings are possible:

- dim: Dim lights

- normal

- washed: Bathed very bright, in light

No firm Lux values are established as many devices are too different and have their own contrast adjustment technologies (e-ink remains readable in bright light, while liquid crystal displays do not provide more contrast). Since brightness sensors are not often calibrated, the result is difficult to predict.

```
1    @media (light-level: normal) {
2        p {
3            background: url("texture.jpg");
4            color: #333 }
5    }
6    @media (light-level: dim) {
```

```
 7     p {
 8        background: #222;
 9        color: #ccc }
10     }
11   @media (light-level: washed) {
12     p {
13        background: white;
14        color: black;
15        font-size: 2em; }
16   }
```

The feature pointer (arrow) changes the accuracy of the indication. Otherwise it is often difficult to distinguish between touch devices on the one hand (smartphones and tablets, as well as consoles like the Wii) and devices with a mouse, touchpad or digital pen are taken. The following settings are possible:

- fine: For devices with mouse, touchpad or stylus

- coarse: For devices with touch or gesture control

- none: Only keyboard input possible

```
1   @media (pointer: coarse) {
2     input {
3       padding 1em;
4       font-size: 2em;
5     }
6   }
```

With touch devices, the font size and the padding of the input field are increased accordingly.

Because most devices have multiple input options, their use can not be predicted. It is possible to use any-pointer to find out whether there is any input device at all.

You can use `pointer` and `any-pointer` if you are unsure of certain devices. However, you can ascertain this in combination with the display width whether someone is on the go via smartphone or tablet, or at home with a desktop computer. This allows you to optimize web pages for specific devices accurately.

The feature `resolution` describes the resolution, which is the density of the pixels on an output medium. If the output medium does not use rectangular pixels (for example, printers), the characteristic may be used only in conjunction with a prefix.

In this case, consider queries with `min-resolution` the lowest possible, queries with `max-resolution` the highest possible density of the pixels of the output medium.

```
1   @media (resolution: 96dpi) {
2     /* The resolution is 96 pixels per inch */
3   }
4   @media (min-resolution: 200dpcm) {
5     /* The resolution is at least 200 points per cm */
6   }
7   @media (max-resolution: 300dpi) {
8     /* The resolution is a maximum of 300 dots per inch */
9   }
```

The feature `scan` describes the screen layout of output devices of the type *tv*. This can be done progressively, which is approximately the screen layout on a computer screen. Allowed values are `progressive` or `interlace`. The value applies to `progressive`, or by means of banding (e.g., individual image lines are gradually displayed), and then applies the value `interlace` to it.

```
1   @media (scan: progressive) {
2     /* Screen Layout  */
3   }
```

The feature grid (height) describes the scanning feature of output media. If output devices that represent the contents in a grid, apply the value one (1), otherwise the value zero (0).

```
1   @media (grid: 0) {
2      /* Numerous font formatting */
3   }
```

The Viewport

Among the foundations of development for mobile devices is the meta-element viewport. This one-line of HTML code ensures a correct scaling of the site on the first call of a device. This is especially useful for mobile devices, where the user's ability to create a custom setting is somehow limited.

The browser of the mobile device goes to mobile view first, even if assuming that sites are not designed for it and the site-wide display width exceeds considerably the available space. The browser viewport (the display area) is therefore set, for example, in Mobile Safari to a width of 980 pixels, so that most sites are fully visible. This has the disadvantage that the content is very small, and fonts are illegible. The user must zoom in to see anything.

Setting Viewport

The adjustment of the viewport can be very easily customized via an HTML element. You can adjust the viewport of any web site that does not have a standard width. This way you can ensure that content and display area match for narrower layouts, so no unnecessary space is wasted. The site will be shown in the maximum possible size. As seen in Figure 2-4, the left side shows *apple.com* on a desktop and the right side shows the zoomed section with larger words.

Figure 2-4. *Web site with and without zoom*

For proper adjustment of the viewport, add the following line in the header of the page. This is then evaluated by mobile devices:

```
1    <!DOCTYPE html>
2    <head>
3        <meta name="viewport" content="width=1024" />
4    </head>
5    <body>
6    </body>
```

If the site is specifically created or optimized for mobile devices, you do not have to specify a fixed width for the viewport. For example, in portrait format a smartphone has a logical width of 320px, and 480px in landscape mode (physically, the value will be higher). This would mean that the same content would be shown only in a different zoom level in portrait and landscape modes.

Instead, a formula is used to convert the modes:

```
1    Width of the Viewport = Width of Device
```

67

The smartphone now has a width of 320px in portrait orientation, so precisely 320px on the site are shown (1:1 ratio). Likewise, 480px will then be shown in landscape orientation. This flexible approach is both device-independent and allows the landscape to have the extra space that makes sense in width.

Figure 2-5 demonstrates the effect. It shows a mobile device with a meta-element in the source code *width=device-width* (left) and without (right).

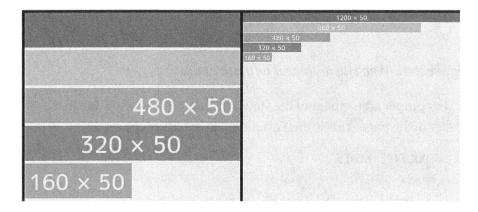

Figure 2-5. *View with and without meta-element*

Viewport Settings

In addition to the *width*, the meta-element for the viewport has more properties that are listed comma-separated:

```
1   <meta name="viewport" content="width=device-width,
2                                   initial-scale=1.0,
3                                   user-scalable=no" />
```

- `initial-scale`: The value specifies the initial zoom level. A 1.0 means that the content of 1:1 will be shown. For example, on a screen with 320 px, a 320 px-wide graphics fills the entire width (see also the screenshot in Figure 2-3). Therefore, a 2.0 results in a 2 times magnification.

- `user-scalable`: With this attribute, you can define whether the user can zoom in on the page (yes) or not (no).

- `minimum-scale` and `maximum-scale`: These two properties you make it possible to limit the zoom level. Set the maximum scale to 2.0, the content can be increased maximum 2 times.

Summary

This chapter covered the basics of CSS and how the system of rules, selectors, and properties works. Because Bootstrap makes use of the flexbox grid models, the related rules are explained more thoroughly. However, the intention was to peek behind the curtain and not to give all details of CSS, because Bootstrap takes care of these details and obstacles for you.

CHAPTER 3

Structure of the Page

Bootstrap constructs a horizontal grid on the page, and the elements are placed within. This is the fundamental part of the framework, and how to deal with the grid and its options is the first decision you make in your project.

Basis for the Grid

The basis for the grid is a fixed allocation of the page. There are several options to distribute elements, centered or not, dealing with overflows and handling breakpoints for different screen resolutions.

The first step is to adjust the web site to HTML5. This is accomplished with the correct doctype:

```
1   <!DOCTYPE html>
2   <html lang="en">
3       ...
4   </html>
```

The Overall Structure of a Page

In general, Bootstrap does not force you to use a particular page design. It is, however, recommended that you follow some pattern. For content pages it might look like the following:

© Jörg Krause 2020
J. Krause, *Introducing Bootstrap 4*, https://doi.org/10.1007/978-1-4842-6203-0_3

Listing 3-1. A HTML 5 Content Page

```
1    <!DOCTYPE html>
2    <html lang="en">
3      <head>
4        <title>Your page's heading</title>
5        <!-- meta data and script inclusion goes here -->
6      </head>
7      <body>
8        <header>
9          <nav>
10           <ul>
11             <li>Your menu</li>
12           </ul>
13         </nav>
14       </header>
15
16       <section>
17
18         <article>
19           <header>
20             <h2>Article Name</h2>
21             <p>Posted on <time datetime="2009-09-
                 04T16:31:24+02:00">September 29th 2016</time> by
                 <a href="#">yourself</a> - <a href="#comments">2
                 comments</a></p>
22           </header>
23           <p>And here the text goes</p>
24         </article>
25
26       </section>
27
```

```
28      <aside>
29        <h2>About</h2>
30        <p>Describe your company here.</p>
31      </aside>
32
33      <footer>
34        <p>Copyright 2016 &copy;</p>
35      </footer>
36    </body>
37  </html>
```

Settings of the Viewing Area

For mobile devices that were supported from the outset, the viewport is now set. The first element at the <head>-section is therefore the following metatag:

```
1   <meta name="viewport"
2        content="width=device-width, initial-scale=1,
         shrink-to-fit=no" />
```

A definitely requirement here is that the zoom behavior and the scale be used at the beginning. The zoom behavior can be turned off with user-scalable=no. The application then feels a little like a native app on a mobile device. shrink-to-fit is specific for Safari browsers on Apple devices (especially iPads), and helps to prevent the device from applying smart zooming, which usually makes things worse.

Zoom Switch Off   It is risky to switch off the zoom function. Users with limited eyesight or users of especially small screens may be reliant upon it. When a mobile web site needs to behave like a native app, it must also be built from the ground as an app.

```
1    <meta name="viewport"
2         content="width=device-width,
3                  initial-scale=1,
4                  maximum-scale=1,
5                  user-scalable=no">
```

The Grid System

In the early years of the Web there was an attempt to provide a kind of virtual grid to give structure to a page. Most often, tables were used. However, tables are rigid in their horizontal extension because the content determines the width. A scaling to a smaller screen is not possible.

The idea of the table shows the procedure, rather than simply having the cells take <div>-tags and then define these grid-like, using CSS. Anyone who has tried it may have quickly realized that the approach is anything but trivial. CSS frameworks therefore provide a solid foundation. In fact, the screen is divided into grids where the grid width can be adapted.

Container

Bootstrap utilizes a container class to initiate the page and find a basis for the grid. Containers can be used multiple times on the page, but should not be nested.

```
1    <div class="container">
2      ...
3    </div>
```

Containers of this type provide a solid, centered, and responsive grid. That is, the width adapts in the device's viewport and then remains stable within a range. The effect is a jump to a new positioning once the range is left or reached. These jump areas are referred to as "breakpoints." If you already know the concept of software development, note that the breakpoints in Bootstrap have nothing in common with this.

As alternative to *container*, the class *.container-fluid* can be used, which always uses the full width of the device's viewport:

```
1   <div class="container-fluid">
2     ...
3   </div>
```

A combination of both is available to provide a full-width view for smaller screens, and falls back to breakpoints if there is enough spaces. Table 3-1 shows the possible dimensions:

Table 3-1. *Control Grid Behavior with Breakpoints*

	Extra small 576px	Small ≥576px	Medium ≥768px	Large ≥992px	Extra large ≥1200px
.container	100%	540px	720px	960px	1140px
.container-sm	100%	540px	720px	960px	1140px
.container-md	100%	100%	720px	960px	1140px
.container-lg	100%	100%	100%	960px	1140px
.container-xl	100%	100%	100%	100%	1140px
.container-fluid	100%	100%	100%	100%	100%

The Grid in Detail

The grid is formed by twelve (12) equal width columns. Predefined classes can be used to place elements on a given column and span a number of columns at a time.

The elements are placed in the columns. Eventually the last column is reached, either by a number of elements or elements that span more than one column. The entirety is called a row. After that, a new row begins. Quite often you will control such rows without the need to fill up all columns. That's why we use *.row* classes.

The procedure should be based on a few rules:

- Rows (*.row*) must be in a container *.container* (fixed width) or *.container-fluid* (full width).

- Rows may be used horizontally to place multiple elements side by side.

- Columns (*.col-xx-n*) may be placed in rows. Only column elements are immediate child elements of rows.

- Column spacing (gap between columns) are defined using *padding*-rules. These distances are to the left of the first column and the right of the last column with negative intervals (*margin*) balanced. This content is aligned outside of the grid left-aligned equal.

- If the elements need columns that can be placed within a row and exceed the elements' limit of twelve columns, then the whole group will be wrapped.

The structure of the column classes is simple:

- The name begins with *col-*

- The middle part (infix) determines the jurisdiction for screen widths (*xs, sm, md, lg*)—the breakpoints. It can be omitted to get default behavior.

- The number at the end determines the number of grid zones (1 to 12) the column spans.

If you use the class *.col-xs-4*, you have three juxtaposing decorated elements (3 x 4 = 12). The higher (larger device) definition applies until it is overwritten. If you use class combinations such as *col-md-2 col-lg-2*, then "md" is not valid for very large devices.

Device-Specific Definitions

Small units with less than 768px will not be defined separately, because this class of device is already the default. The information contained in the variables are defined as follows:

- "xs": < 576px

- "sm": ≥ 576px and < 768px

- "md": ≥ 768px and < 992px

- "lg": ≥ 992px and < 1200px

- "xl": ≥ 1200px

The following definitions are pulled from the Sass sources using mixins. You can read more about this technique in the appendix about Sass.

```
1   @media (min-width: @screen-sm-min) { ... }
2
3   @media (min-width: @screen-md-min) { ... }
4
5   @media (min-width: @screen-lg-min) { ... }
```

Table 3-2 shows the dimensions of the grid for specific container widths.

Table 3-2. *Position of Breakpoints*

Symbol	Device width	Container	Width
xs	<576px	automatically	automatically
sm	≥576px	750px	62px
md	≥768px	970px	81px
lg	≥992px	1170px	97px
xl	≥1200px	1570px	112px

The width of the spacing between columns is 30 pixels (15 on each side).

In Listing 3-2, only "md" classes are used. These are only valid as of the width of 970px. The div elements are therefore arranged among each other on small devices—only on desktops with sufficient width. The items appear next to each other.

Listing 3-2. Pattern Grid (Grid.html)

```
1    <div class="container">
2      <div class="row">
3        <div class="col-md-1">1</div>
4        <div class="col-md-1">2</div>
5        <div class="col-md-1">3</div>
6        <div class="col-md-1">4</div>
7        <div class="col-md-1">5</div>
8        <div class="col-md-1">6</div>
9        <div class="col-md-1">7</div>
10       <div class="col-md-1">8</div>
11       <div class="col-md-1">9</div>
12       <div class="col-md-1">10</div>
13       <div class="col-md-1">11</div>
14       <div class="col-md-1">12</div>
15     </div>
```

```
16    <div class="row">
17      <div class="col-md-8">1-8</div>
18      <div class="col-md-4">9-12</div>
19    </div>
20    <div class="row">
21      <div class="col-md-4">1-4</div>
22      <div class="col-md-4">5-8</div>
23      <div class="col-md-4">9-12</div>
24    </div>
25    <div class="row">
26      <div class="col-md-6">1-6</div>
27      <div class="col-md-6">7-12</div>
28    </div>
29  </div>
```

With few extra styles to illustrate the areas it looks like Figure 3-1.

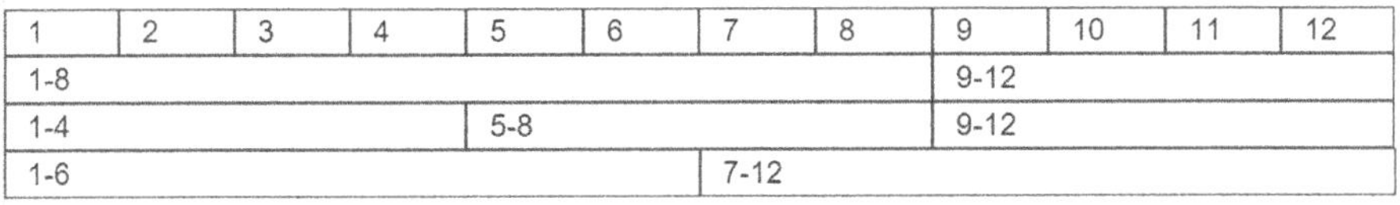

1	2	3	4	5	6	7	8	9	10	11	12
1-8								9-12			
1-4				5-8				9-12			
1-6						7-12					

Figure 3-1. *The grid system (desktop)*

On a mobile device the same code produces the following screen:

| 1 |
| 2 |
| 3 |
| 4 |
| 5 |
| 6 |
| 7 |
| 8 |
| 9 |
| 10 |
| 11 |
| 12 |
| 1-8 |
| 9-12 |
| 1-4 |
| 5-8 |
| 9-12 |
| 1-6 |
| 7-12 |

Figure 3-2. *The grid system (mobile)*

It may happen that mobile devices provide adequate space, or represent some columns side by side. These are further definitions of *.col-xs--* and *.col-md--*added classes.

The first row shows that on small devices every twelve of the first six columns are used. If the screen is bigger only eight or four columns are used (which are then wider). The second set uses 50% of the screen on small devices and 33% on large devices. The third row always uses 50% width, regardless of the size of the device ("sm" scales high when no further definition follows). See Listing 3-3.

Listing 3-3. Pattern Grid (Grid_xs.html)

```
1   <div class="row">
2     <div class="col-sm-12 col-md-8">12 or 8</div>
3     <div class="col-sm-6 col-md-4">6 or 4</div>
4   </div>
5
6   <div class="row">
7     <div class="col-sm-6 col-md-4">50% or 33.4%</div>
8     <div class="col-sm-6 col-md-4">50% or 33.4%</div>
9     <div class="col-sm-6 col-md-4">50% or 33.4%</div>
10  </div>
11
12  <div class="row">
13    <div class="col-sm-6">.col-sm-6</div>
14    <div class="col-sm-6">.col-sm-6</div>
15  </div>
```

On a desktop, the code produces the output as shown in Figure 3-3:

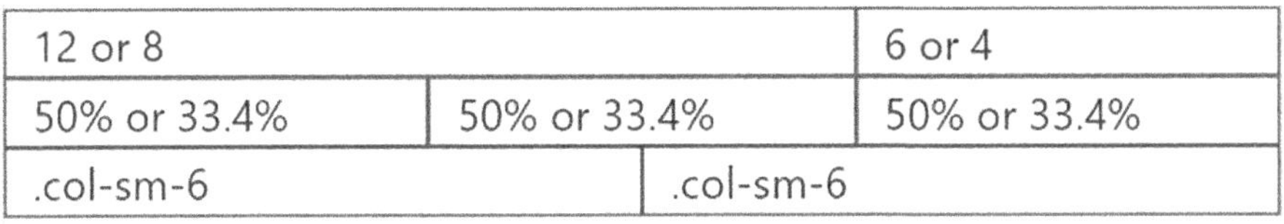

12 or 8		6 or 4	
50% or 33.4%	50% or 33.4%	50% or 33.4%	
.col-sm-6		.col-sm-6	

Figure 3-3. *Variable grid system (desktop)*

On a mobile device the same code (Listing 3-3) produces the output as shown in Figure 3-4:

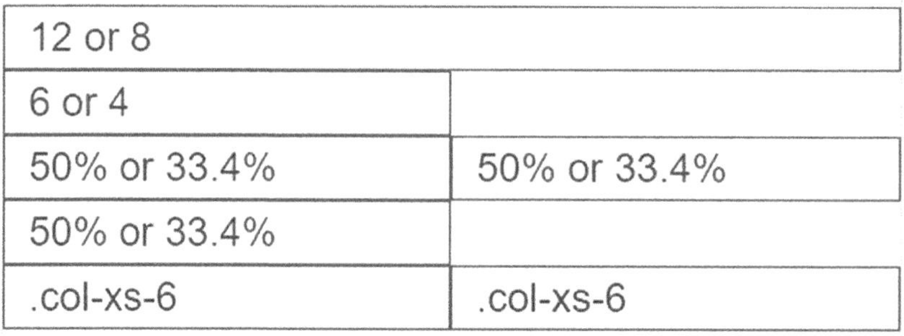

12 or 8	
6 or 4	
50% or 33.4%	50% or 33.4%
50% or 33.4%	
.col-xs-6	.col-xs-6

Figure 3-4. *Variable grid system (mobile)*

If more classes are being used, another gradation is possible. Some tablets, for example, could make use of the variant "sm" explicitly. See the example in Listing 3-4.

Listing 3-4. Grid for Different Devices (Grid_Tablet.html)

```
1   <div class="row">
2     <div class="col-12 col-md-6 col-lg-8">
3       Small: 12 Tablet: 6 Large: 8
4     </div>
5     <div class="col-6 col-md-4">
6       Small: 6 Large: 4
7     </div>
8   </div>
9   <div class="row">
10    <div class="col-6 col-md-4">A Small: 6 Tablet: 4</div>
11    <div class="col-6 col-md-4">B Small: 6 Tablet: 4</div>
12    <div class="col-6 d-md-none">
13      C Small: 6 Tablet: invisible
14    </div>
15  </div>
```

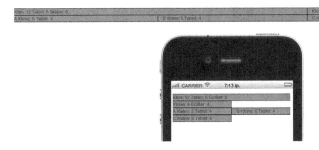

Figure 3-5. *Tablet (top) versus phone*

The limit of 12 columns is not absolute, and contents are never clipped. What does not fit into the grid is simply moved to the next virtual row. Items that are in a column definition will be moved as a whole. Using a nested row with *col-sm-2* and *col-sm-8* doesn't work, because once you are in a twelve-column nested grid the *col-sm-2* is too small, and the *col-sm-8* doesn't go to the end of the row. The page would appear somehow incomplete.

Listing 3-5. Pattern Grid (Grid_Break.html)

```
1   <div class="row">
2     <div class="col-sm-9">9</div>
3     <div class="col-sm-4">4<br>And more content...</div>
4     <div class="col-sm-6">6<br>Then additional columns.</div>
5   </div>
```

In the example in Listing 3-5, nine and four columns are required, but this equals 13 and does not fit twelve-column limit. Therefore, the second element (line 3), spanned by four columns, is moved to the next line. The other element with the six columns simply arrange themselves behind. This results in two rows. The infix "sm" is just an example for small devices; the behavior would appear with any modification. The results can be seen in in Figure 3-6.

83

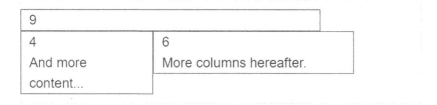

Figure 3-6. *Break off the grid*

Utilizing the Width

To take advantage of the full width, *.container-fluid* is used in Listing 3-6.

Listing 3-6. Offset Use (Grid_Fluid.html)

```
1  <div class="container-fluid">
2    <div class="row">
3      ...
4    </div>
5  </div>
```

The left and right edges of each 15 px is placed so that the item in the container uses the space to the best advantage, as seen in Figure 3-7.

Figure 3-7. *Normal container (top) and with -fluid (bottom)*

In the following examples, I have dispensed with the container element to keep the code compact. But you must use a container element in practice.

Offsets: Moving the Start Column

Offsets move the starting point of a column to the right (see Listing 3-7 for offset use). This is based on the current horizontal position within the grid. Unoccupied columns already move the starting point, so the offset just adds on to this (see Figure 3-8). Used classes are like *.col-xx-offset-* (xx is a placeholder for the base widths of the Media Queries or can be left out as a fallback *.col-offset-*).

Listing 3-7. Offset Use (Grid_Offset.html)

```
1    <div class="row">
2      <div class="col-4">4</div>
3      <div class="col-4 col-offset-4">4 + 4</div>
4    </div>
5    <div class="row">
6      <div class="col-3 col-offset-3">3 + 3</div>
7      <div class="col-3 col-offset-3">3 + 3</div>
8    </div>
9    <div class="row">
10     <div class="col-6 col-offset-3">6 + 3</div>
11   </div>
```

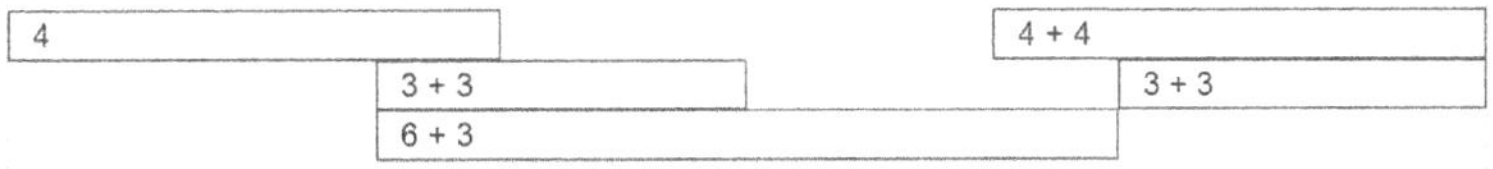

Figure 3-8. *Elements in moving columns*

85

Interlace Columns

Containers must not be nested (see Listing 3-8 and Figure 3-9). However, this is allowed in rows. Therefore, subordinate areas can be created. It is not mandatory that such areas fill out their parent's area, and it must not extend until all twelve columns are used.

Listing 3-8. Offset Use (Grid_Nested.html)

```
1   <div class="row">
2     <div class="col-sm-9">
3       Parent are: 9 columns
4       <div class="row">
5         <div class="col-sm-8 col-md-6">
6           Child 1: 8 or 6
7         </div>
8         <div class="col-sm-4 col-md-6">
9           Child 2: 4 or 6
10        </div>
11      </div>
12    </div>
13  </div>
```

Parent are: 9 columns	
Child 1: 8 or 6	Child 2: 4 or 6

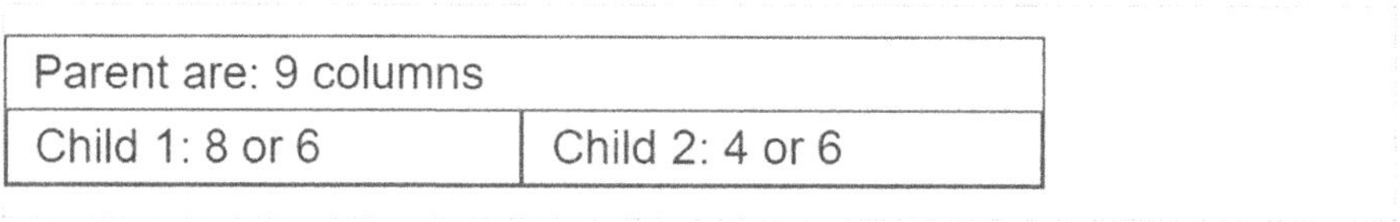

Figure 3-9. *Behavior of nested columns*

Order Columns

If individual columns are to be placed outside their natural order, you can use the class *.order-*, as shown in Listing 3-9. The columns are pushed to the position, which is an ordinal number.

Listing 3-9. Offset Use (Grid_Sorted.html)

```
1   <div class="row">
2     <div class="col-9 order-2">9 + 3 right</div>
3     <div class="col-3 order-1">3 + 9 left</div>
4   </div>
```

The result of Listing 3-8 is shown in Figure 3-10.

3 + 9 left	9 + 3 right

Figure 3-10. *Order with desktop*

If the order was defined only for the size "md," the mobile device falls back to the arrangement in HTML. See Listing 3-10 and Figure 3-11.

Listing 3-10. Offset Use with Breakpoint (Grid_Sorted.html, part 2)

```
1   <div class="row">
2     <div class="col-9 order-md-2">9 + 3 right</div>
3     <div class="col-3 order-md-1">3 + 9 left</div>
4   </div>
```

3 + 9 left	9 + 3 right	
9 + 3 right		3 + 9 left

Figure 3-11. *Sorting on a mobile device (lower part)*

Fallbacks and Utilities

Some utility classes allow a finer control for element placement.

Equal Distribution

There is a class you use if an equal distribution regardless the number or elements is the goal. The grid is still limited to twelve columns. Just use *.col*.

```
1    <div class="row">
2      <div class="col">
3        First one-third
4      </div>
5      <div class="col">
6        Second one-third
7      </div>
8      <div class="col">
9        Third one-third
10     </div>
11   </div>
```

The class can be combined with any of the *.col-* classes shown earlier. *.col-6* will cover six columns, and the *.col* class spans the remaining space and distributes equally in that space. The breakpoints apply, too. Just use classes such as *.col-md*, for example.

Sometimes you need more dynamics and want to stretch columns according to the content's size. Here you can use *.col-auto* classes, whereas *auto* replaces the column number. All breakpoint infixes are available.

Row Columns

The responsive *.row-cols-* classes set the number of columns that best render your content and layout. Whereas normal *.col-* classes apply to the individual columns, the row columns classes are set on the parent *.row*. This is a simplification and reduces the number of <div> elements, but it doesn't provide additional functionality.

Use these row columns classes to quickly create basic grid layouts or to control your card layouts:

```
1   <div class="container">
2     <div class="row row-cols-2">
3       <div class="col">Column</div>
4       <div class="col">Column</div>
5       <div class="col">Column</div>
6       <div class="col">Column</div>
7     </div>
8   </div>
```

Alignments

The grid in Bootstrap 4 makes use of the flexbox (flex model) capabilities (discussed Chapter 2). Therefore, the ability to align elements within containers has been greatly improved, as shown in Listing 3-11.

Listing 3-11. Vertical Alignment (Grid_Alignment.html2)

```
1   <div class="col">
2     One of three columns
3   </div>
4   <div class="col">
5     One of three columns
6   </div>
```

```
 7   <div class="col">
 8      One of three columns
 9   </div>
10   <div class="col">
11      One of three columns
12   </div>
13   <div class="col">
14      One of three columns
15   </div>
16   <div class="col">
17      One of three columns
18   </div>
19   <div class="col">
20      One of three columns
21   </div>
22   <div class="col">
23      One of three columns
24   </div>
25   <div class="col">
26      One of three columns
27   </div>
```

Listing 3-10 has an additional style to increase the row height so that there is a visible effect. In reality the content would stretch the elements. If the content isn't able to do this, the effect might remain invisible. The screenshot in Figure 3-12 has additional border colors for the purpose of explanation.

One of three columns	One of three columns	One of three columns

One of three columns	One of three columns	One of three columns

One of three columns	One of three columns	One of three columns

Figure 3-12. *Align in rows vertically*

Just like the vertical alignment, the elements can also be aligned horizontally. That's rarely an issue, because of the other alignment and offset options. However, in case an element has to be put specifically left, right, or centered, some special classes apply. Use *.justify-content-<pos>* with of these position fields:

- *start*: columns start left
- *center*: columns are centered
- *end*: columns align to the right
- *around*: columns are around a center
- *between*: columns are split to end and start (remaining content is between)

Note that the effect is invisible if all columns are occupied. The alignment makes sense if you have less than twelve columns in a grid of twelve ones. You may also have noticed that the terms "start" and "end" are used, and applies to "left" and "right." In layouts with different writing direction order, "rtl" (right to left, such as Arabic) the "start" and "end" terms still apply. But "left" and "right" would be the opposite, which would be confusing.

Auxiliary Classes

Some helper classes are available to deal more directly with the grid, especially the flexbox model.

The Flex Classes

The classes in this realm do not completely replace the common flexbox rules. That wouldn't make sense, as the options are many and the effort to learn new names contradicts the advantage of having a common style system. But for simple flexbox applications, it could be easier to use Bootstrap.

Flexbox classes start with *.d-flex*. There is another option for inline elements, *.d-inline-flex*. All the flex classes are aware of breakpoints, provided as an infix (in the middle):

```
1   .d-sm-flex
2   .d-xl-inline-flex
```

After creating a box using this, you can apply the row behavior using *.flex-row*. If you like to have a vertical flow, just use *.flex-column* or *.flex-column-reverse*. Even for these, the breakpoint infixes are applicable.

If the items do not fill the available space you should define the alignment (vertically) and justification (horizontally). The base classes are shown here:

```
1   <div class="d-flex justify-content-start">...</div>
2   <div class="d-flex justify-content-end">...</div>
3   <div class="d-flex justify-content-center">...</div>
4   <div class="d-flex justify-content-between">...</div>
5   <div class="d-flex justify-content-around">...</div>
```

After "justify-content," the breakpoint infix can be added (e.g., *justify-content-sm-around*). For the alignment it looks like this:

```
1   <div class="d-flex align-items-start">...</div>
2   <div class="d-flex align-items-end">...</div>
3   <div class="d-flex align-items-center">...</div>
4   <div class="d-flex align-items-baseline">...</div>
5   <div class="d-flex align-items-stretch">...</div>
```

Within the Flexbox

Within the flexbox you can modify the items in various ways. Use one of these variants (all can have breakpoints additionally):

- *.flex-fill*: stretch the items to fill the available space.

- *.flex-grow*: let one element grow and the others remain in their natural size.

- *.flex-shrink*: let one shrink as much as possible and the others remain in their natural size.

- *.flex-wrap* and *.flex-nowrap*: control weather the elements wrap when reaching the box' borders.

- *.order-{n}*: change the items order with the number between 1 and 12.

Summary

This chapter covered the basic page layout, the grid, and the alignment of elements within. Some classes help to modify this layout, and you can also use common flex classes to create your own grid.

CHAPTER 4

Typography

Bootstrap defines styles for some HTML elements directly, such as the basic type of appearance, typography, and color. In contrast to the classic concept of typography, font, writing, design, and printing material, Bootstrap is quite modest in its ease of use. The following are specifically regulated:

- The background color of the page is white, `background-color: #fff`

- In the Sass files the following variables are responsible for the basic design:

  - `$font-family-base`

  - `$font-size-base`

  - `$line-height-base`

- Hyperlinks as outstanding elements of web pages are determined by the following variables:

  - `$link-color`

- Underline links should only be used with floating cursor (`:hover`)

The variables are in the file *_scaffolding.sass* and are easy to find.

© Jörg Krause 2020
J. Krause, *Introducing Bootstrap 4*, https://doi.org/10.1007/978-1-4842-6203-0_4

Headings

All headings from <h1> to <h6> are directly supported. You must not use any other classes. But if you wish to use the same font size as a heading, the text should use the classes *.h1* to *.h6*. See Figure 4-1 for an example of headings.

- h1: Bold 2.5 rem / 40 px (Basis × 2.6)

- h2: Bold 2 rem / 32 px (Basis × 2.15)

- h3: Bold 1.75 rem / 28 px (Basis × 1.7)

- h4: Bold 1.5 rem / 24 px (Basis × 1.25)

- h5: Bold 1.25 rem / 20 px (standard size, this is the basis for calculation)

- h6: Bold 1 rem / 16 px (Basis × 0.85)

```
1   <h1>h1. Bootstrap Heading</h1>
2   <h2>h2. Bootstrap Heading</h2>
3   <h3>h3. Bootstrap Heading</h3>
4   <h4>h4. Bootstrap Heading</h4>
5   <h5>h5. Bootstrap Heading</h5>
6   <h6>h6. Bootstrap Heading</h6>
```

To obtain a lighter (smaller, lighter) appearance, use <small> or .small, as in Listing 4-1:

Listing 4-1. Heading Styles (Typo_Heading.html)

```
1   <h1>h1. Bootstrap Heading <small>Additional text</small></h1>
2   <h2>h2. Bootstrap Heading <small>Additional text</small></h2>
3   <h3>h3. Bootstrap Heading <small>Additional text</small></h3>
4   <h4>h4. Bootstrap Heading <small>Additional text</small></h4>
5   <h5>h5. Bootstrap Heading <small>Additional text</small></h5>
6   <h6>h6. Bootstrap Heading <small>Additional text</small></h6>
```

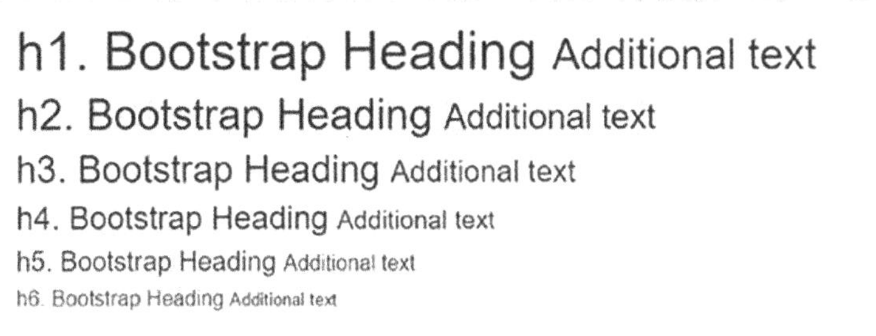

h1. Bootstrap Heading Additional text

h2. Bootstrap Heading Additional text

h3. Bootstrap Heading Additional text

h4. Bootstrap Heading Additional text

h5. Bootstrap Heading Additional text

h6. Bootstrap Heading Additional text

Figure 4-1. *Standard view of headings*

Display Headings

An alternative form of heading styles comes with the display classes. There are only four such heading styles. The class names are .display-1, .display-2, and so on. The font is slightly larger and the display headings stands a bit more out compared with the regular headings.

The interesting part here is that the actual element doesn't matter. Whether you apply these classes to a <div> element or even <h1>, the result is the same (see Figure 4-2).

Display 1
Display 2
Display 3
Display 4

Figure 4-2. *Display headings based on div*

Text and Text Elements

For text and text elements, HTML has many references and has class supplements for special effects.

Basic Font

The default font for the text is 16 px. The line height used is 1.15. Sections created with <p> will receive half the row height, about 10 px.

To single out one section, the class .lead is used as shown in Figure 4-3.

```
1   <p class="lead">Important paragraph...</p>
2   <p>Standard paragraph </p>
```

Important paragraph...

Standard paragraph

Figure 4-3. *Paragraph style*

Text Elements

Text elements are used for parts of the body text. This is done mainly through HTML and not classes. The elements also serve to strengthen the semantic content. Figure 4-4 shows various semantic elements in the text. The following text elements are explicitly supported:

- `<mark></mark>`

  This text is highlighted (as with a highlighter) emphasizing relevance.

- `<del></del>`

This indicates that a part of the text has been deleted, which is indicated by a strikethrough.

- `<s></s>`

  This indicates that a part of the text is no longer relevant.

- `<ins></ins>`

  This tag indicates that the body part has been added allowing a user to signal a last text change.

- `<u></u>`

  This tag indicates by underlining that the text provides additional information.

- `<em></em>`

  Highlights part of the text with emphasis thereby showing its importance.

Another tag fits in this category, `<small></small>`, but it has a less important semantic reference. To achieve a lighter display you can reduce the font size to 85%. To do the opposite of this, you should use `<strong></strong>`.

Bootstrap supports the continued nonsemantic elements `<b></b>` and `<i></i>`. They react in the text similar to `<strong></strong>` and `<em></em>`. The element `<i></i>` is sometimes is used for icons, which do not contain text and therefore ignore the behavior displayed by italic font and enter an element with a certain semantic meaning. However, the behavior and the interpretation is not standard compliant, but more of a stylistic measure.

Some elements are marked more semantically.

```
1    <abbr title="Abbreviation">Abbr.</abbr>
```

This element identifies abbreviations, but an attribute title is required. The element is marked with a dotted underline and displays the title when the mouse pointer hovers over it. In addition, the font can be reduced with the class *.initialism* to have a less disruptive effect in the text.

```
1    <abbr title="HyperText Markup Language"
2    class="initialism">HTML</abbr>
```

The `<kbd></kbd>` element is used to refer to keys of a computer keyboard (`<kbd>F12</kbd>`).

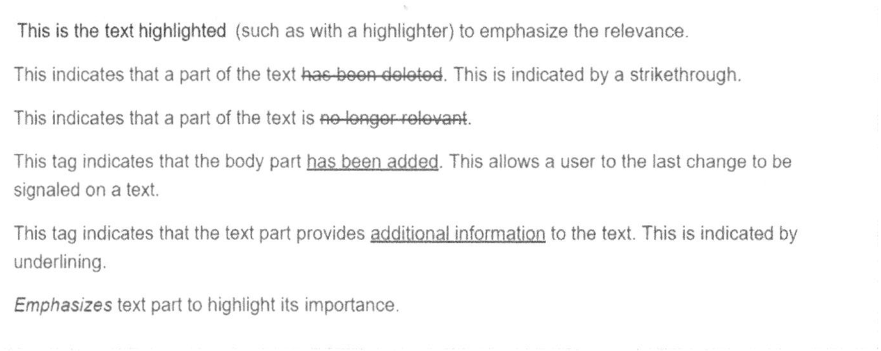

This is the text highlighted (such as with a highlighter) to emphasize the relevance.

This indicates that a part of the text has been deleted. This is indicated by a strikethrough.

This indicates that a part of the text is no longer relevant.

This tag indicates that the body part has been added. This allows a user to the last change to be signaled on a text.

This tag indicates that the text part provides additional information to the text. This is indicated by underlining.

Emphasizes text part to highlight its importance.

Figure 4-4. *Semantic elements in the text*

Elements for Text Blocks

The element `<address></address>` can make it easy to detect addresses. This element is not formatted. If formatting is to be retained, additional line breaks with `<br/>` elements are required. See Figure 4-5 for a correctly formatted address.

```
1    <address>
2      <strong>Twitter, Inc.</strong><br>
3      795 Folsom Ave, Suite 600<br>
```

```
4    San Francisco, CA 94107<br>
5    <abbr title="Phone">P:</abbr> (123) 456-7890
6  </address>
```

Twitter, Inc.
795 Folsom Ave, Suite 600
San Francisco, CA 94107
P: (123) 456-7890
[Phone]

Figure 4-5. *A properly formatted address*

The content of the element <address></address> is not limited to an actual address. You can put in anything similar.

```
1  <address>
2  <strong>Full Name</strong><br>
3  <a href="mailto:#">first.last@example.com</a>
4  </address>
```

Quotes (<blockquote>) are also semantic and highlight text that refers to something else, such as a quote.

```
1  <blockquote class="blockquote">
2    <p>Node.js is a modern programming environment.</p>
3  </blockquote>
```

For the referenced text, if you add the element <cite></cite>, the text is then highlighted. The element <footer></footer> indicates the source.

```
1  <blockquote class="blockquote">
2    <p>Node.js is a modern programming environment.</p>
3    <footer class="blockquote-footer">Found in
4     <cite title="Introduction to Node,js">Node.js</cite>
5    </footer>
6  </blockquote>
```

On some screens quotes are not immediately recognizable. They are aligned to the right, so structuring them to the side may help (see Figure 4-6 for a right-aligned quote).

Node.js is a modern programming environment.

— Found in *Node.js*

Node.js is a modern programming environment.

Found in *Node.js* —

Figure 4-6. *Left- and right-aligned quote*

This is the purpose of the class .blockquote-reverse.

```
1    <blockquote class="blockquote-reverse">
2    ...
3    </blockquote>
```

Often code is explained on web pages. This will fit best in <code> </code> and when it is in a row and in <pre></pre>, the formatting will be maintained over several lines. If you need to refer to variables in the text use the element <var></var>. Use this element in mathematical formulas as well as in the following example and in Figure 4-7.

```
1    <var>f(x)</var> = <var>m</var><var>x</var> + <var>b</var>
```

$$f(x) = mx + b$$

Figure 4-7. *Display of variables or formulas*

To explain sample output from a program you should use the element <samp></samp>.

Alignment and Wrapping

The alignment of text is up to your creative nature.

- *text-left*: left-aligned

- *text-center*: text is centered

- *text-right*: right-aligned

- *text-justify*: justified

- *text-nowrap*: obstruction of upheaval; in addition, there are alignment variants that are only valid for certain viewports.

- *text-xs-left*: left-aligned when the viewport "xs" is used.

- *text-xs-center*: text is centered when the viewport "xs" is used.

- *text-xs-right*: right-aligned when the viewport "xs" is used.

This also applies for "sm," "md," "lg," and "xl." Listing 4-2 and Figure 4-8 demonstrate some text alignments.

Listing 4-2. Alignment of Text (Typo_TextAlign.html)

```
1   <p class="text-left">Left aligned.</p>
2   <p class="text-center">Text is centered. </p>
3   <p class="text-right">Right aligned.</p>
4   <p class="text-justify">Justified ...</p>
5   <p class="text-nowrap">Obstruction of Upheaval, ...</p>
```

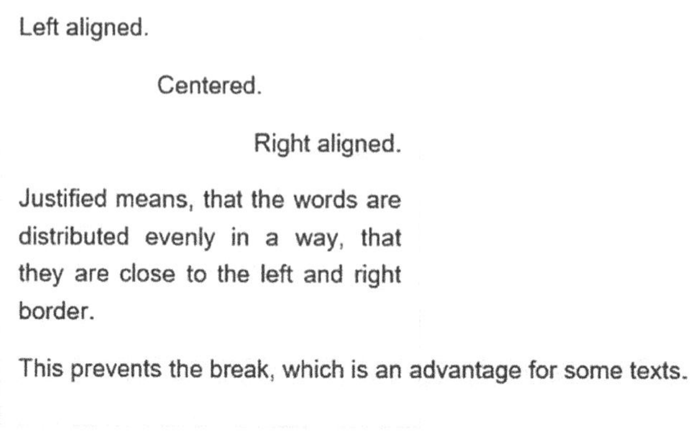

Left aligned.

Centered.

Right aligned.

Justified means, that the words are distributed evenly in a way, that they are close to the left and right border.

This prevents the break, which is an advantage for some texts.

Figure 4-8. *Aligning text*

Justified   Justified (justify) text on screens is generally not a good idea. If you feel the need for justification, remember that the width of the column can hold at least 10 words; otherwise, the spaces between the words become too large. Although justification does not work well, it can remain manageable by using artificial separations with the entity &shy (soft hyphen). The delimiters appear only if a break must be made.

Text Transformations

Transformations convert text from lowercase to uppercase and vice versa. Listing 4-3 and Figure 4-9 provide information on transformations.

- *text-lowercase*: converts to lowercase.

- *text-uppercase*: converts to uppercase.

- *text-capitalize*: first letter of each word is capitalized.

- *text-weight-bold*: bold without an explicit tag.

- *text-weight-normal*: normal weight without an explicit tag.

- *text-italics*: italics without an explicit tag.

Listing 4-3. Transformations (Typo_TextTransform.html)

```
1    <p class="text-lowercase">lowercase</p>
2    <p class="text-uppercase">uppercase</p>
3    <p class="text-capitalize">title case</p>
```

lower case

UPPER CASE

The Title

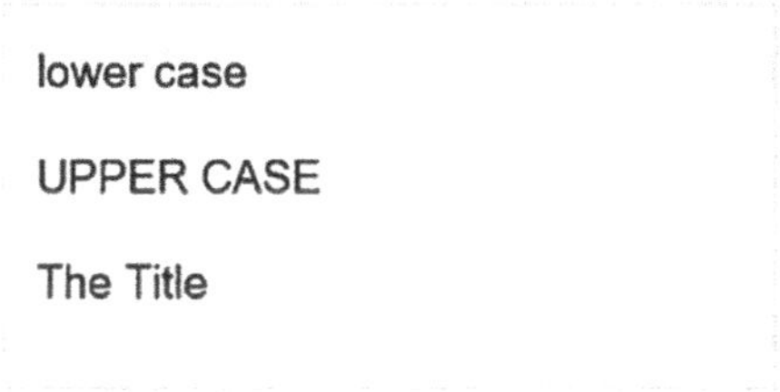

Figure 4-9. *Text transformation*

Lists

There are two types of lists: with order and in no particular order. Without order they are represented in HTML by bullet points. In Bootstrap you can also waive these symbols and create a simple "element stack."

```
1    <ul>
2    <li>...</li>
3    </ul>
```

Lists with order decorate the elements with consecutive numbers, letters, or roman numerals.

```
1   <ol>
2   <li>...</li>
3   </ol>
```

If the default style is used and there are icons that are not needed, they can be removed by the class .list-unstyled. This will affect only the immediate members and not the deeper nesting levels. Note here that the removal of the symbols means that the items are no longer engaged. This must be offset by a distance where appropriate.

```
1   <ul class="list-unstyled">
2   <li>...</li>
3   </ul>
```

These are often defined as lists, and then lose that nature by CSS. The advantage over tables or definition lists is their particularly compact notation—usually two letters per element. The class .list-inline is then necessary to place the elements in horizontal direction (see Figure 4-10).

```
1   <ul class="list-inline">
2   <li>...</li>
3   </ul>
```

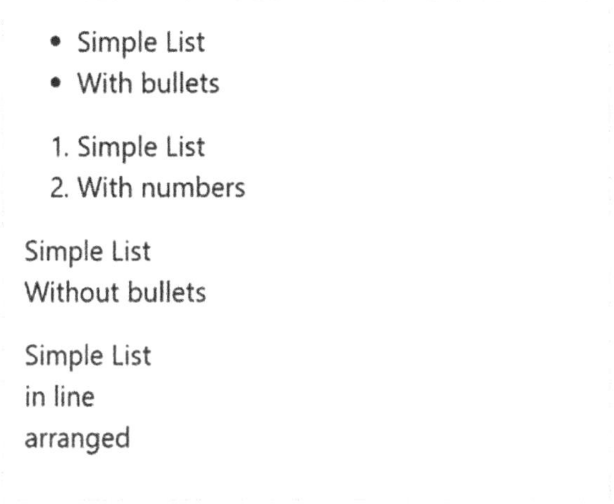

- Simple List
- With bullets

1. Simple List
2. With numbers

Simple List
Without bullets

Simple List
in line
arranged

Figure 4-10. *Some styled lists*

If lists are complex, a suitable replacement is a definition list. Here two blocks per entry are actually used—the term (definition term, <dt></dt>) and the description (definition description, <dd></dd>). Listing 4-4 shows a list definition.

Listing 4-4. List Definition (Typo_Definition.html)

```
1   <dl>
2     <dt>...</dt>
3     <dd>...</dd>
4   </dl>
```

As with simple lists, elements also can be arranged horizontally; in each case the <dt>-element is aligned to the right and the right <dd>-element then left-justified. To align definitions simply put the definition in a .row class and define the size with regular column classes.

```
1   <dl class="row">
2     <dt class="col-md-2">Name</dt>
3     <dd class="col-md-4">Anton Muller</dd>
```

```
4     <dt class="col-md-2">Address</dt>
5     <dd class="col-md-4">NYC</dd>
6   </dl>
```

The <dl>-sections are always set among themselves, as shown in Figure 4-11. Terms that do not fit in the display area are truncated.

HTML
Hypertext Markup Language

CSS
Cascading Style Sheets

Name   Anton Muller

Address   NYC

Figure 4-11. *Assembly with two entries (vertically above, horizontally below)*

Tables

It has been noted that tables are not suited to building responsive sites. Nevertheless, tables are suited for sorting and listing data. The width of the table must comply with the criteria of the grid. A placement outside of the grid is possible. In this case Bootstrap offers several styles to improve the presentation. For responsive environments, tables are offered with horizontal scrolling. Of course this is only a temporary solution; responsive tables should not need this.

Styles for Tables

Tables themselves have a native element in HTML. Nevertheless, Bootstrap relies on the class *.table*. This is because tables are used by many other libraries and plug-ins, such as Calendar. To avoid changes to these tables accidentally by Bootstrap this additional class is required.

```
1    <table class="table">
2      ...
3    </table>
```

Tables consist of three parts: header (<thead></thead>), content (<tbody></tbody>), and footer (<tfoot></tfoot>). The content can occasionally be very long. The readability can be significantly increased by an alternating background color called the "crosswalk effect." You can reach it with the class .table-striped. Figure 4-12 gives an example of such a table.

```
1    <table class="table table-striped">
2      ...
3    </table>
```

Another style for the table is .table-bordered, where a frame is applied to all the cells.

```
1    <table class="table table-bordered">
2      ...
3    </table>
```

More interactive is .table-hover, which shows a mouse effect when hovering over rows of a table.

```
1    <table class="table table-hover">
2      ...
3    </table>
```

If space is in short supply, the distances used by the default can be reduced with *.table-sm.* The table can be reduced by 50%.

```
1   <table class="table table-sm">
2   ...
3   </table>
```

Name	Action
Anton Muller	Edit | Delete
Bob Thornten	Edit | Delete
Britney Belle	Edit | Delete
	2

Figure 4-12. *A table that is partly condensed with header and footer*

Columns   Tables also can have column definitions with `<colgroup><col><col></colgroup>` elements. However, those are not explicitly supported by Bootstrap.

To achieve similar effects such as alternating row colors for columns instead of rows, the following CSS code could serve (the colors are examples):

```
1   colgroup col.success {
2   background-color: #dff0d8;
3   }
4   colgroup col.error {
5   background-color: #f2dede;
6   }
```

```
 7  colgroup col.warning {
 8  background-color: #fcf8e3;
 9  }
10  colgroup col.info {
11  background-color: #d9edf7;
12  }
```

The example refers to the context classes that act as follows.

- *.active*: mouse effect for rows or cells.

- *.success*: positive or success (green).

- *.info*: information or action (blue).

- *.warning*: warning or caution signal (orange).

- *.danger*: negative or danger (red).

```
 1  <!-- Rows -->
 2  <tr class="active">...</tr>
 3  <tr class="success">...</tr>
 4  <tr class="warning">...</tr>
 5  <tr class="danger">...</tr>
 6  <tr class="info">...</tr>
 7
 8  <!-- Cells (td or th) -->
 9  <tr>
10  <td class="active">...</td>
11  <td class="success">...</td>
12  <td class="warning">...</td>
13  <td class="danger">...</td>
14  <td class="info">...</td>
15  </tr>
```

The headings of the table are then referenced on the column elements. Figure 4-13 shows a table with column definitions.

```
1   <table class="table table-bordered table-sm">
2   <colgroup>
3   <col class="success" />
4   <col class="warning" />
5   </colgroup> 6      ...
```

Figure 4-13. Table with column definitions

Note that even the column styles collide with .table-striped. Avoid .table-striped if your columns make color variations.

Legibility for Screen Readers   If a page is built accessibly, the context classes have no meaning. The potentially important information that arises from the choice of color is lost. Therefore, when you add additional items, you can mark these with *.sr-only* to make them invisible. Screen readers will still read these items.

New in Bootstrap 4

There are new classes in Bootstrap 4: *.table-inverse* or *.thead-inverse*, to invert the font color. Figure 4-14 shows an inverted table.

```
1    <table class="table table-inverse" >
2        <thead>
3          <tr>
4            <th>Code</th>
5            <th>Company</th>
6            <th>Price</th>
7            <th>Change</th>
8            <th>In %</th>
9            <th>Opening</th>
10           <th>Highest</th>
11           <th>Lowest</th>
12           <th>Volume</th>
13         </tr>
14       </thead>
15       <tbody>
16         <tr>
17           <td>MSC</td>
18           <td>Microsoft</td>
19           ...
```

Code	Company	Price	Change	In %	Opening	Max	Min	Volume
MSC	Microsoft	$1.38	-0.01	-0.36%	$1.39	$1.39	$1.38	9,395
APP	Apple	$1.99	-0.03	-0.45%	$1.88	$2.15	$1.38	7,741

Figure 4-14. *An inverted table*

113

Particularly interesting is .table-reflow. Using this the block of headlines on the first column is transformed as a pivot table.

```
1    <table class="table " >
2            <thead>
3              <tr>
4                <th>Code</th>
5                <th>Company</th>
6                <th>Price</th>
7                <th>Change</th>
8                <th>In %</th>
9                <th>Opening</th>
10               <th>Highest</th>
11               <th>Lowest</th>
12               <th>Volume</th>
13             </tr>
14           </thead>
15           <tbody>
16             <tr>
17               <td>MSC</td>
18               <td>Microsoft</td>
19           ...
```

For this effect, no modification of the table structure is required (see this effect in Figure 4-15).

Code	MSC	APP
Company	Microsoft	Apple
Price	$1.38	$1.99
Change	-0.01	-0.03
In %	-0.36%	-0.45%
Opening	$1.39	$1.88
Max	$1.39	$2.15
Min	$1.38	$1.38
Volume	9,395	7,741

Figure 4-15. *A turned table*

Responsive Tables

In the strictest sense, responsive tables do not exist. If .table-responsive is used, especially in widths below 768 px, a horizontal scrollbar under the table is created. Figure 4-16 shows a table with a horizontal scrollbar. This will prevent the need for the entire page to scroll horizontally. In addition, it prevents overflow: hidden suppresses all elements that will protrude upward or downward from the table. Caution: This can break or shorten menus or lists and disturb the grid.

```
1   <table class="table table-responsive">
2     ...
3   </table>
```

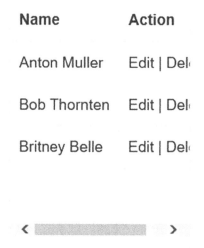

Figure 4-16. *Table with scrollbar*

Note   You no longer need to apply *.table-responsive* as you did with Bootstrap 3 on a surrounding <div>- element.

True Responsive Tables

Bootstrap's responsive answer to tables with *.table-reflow* is not always satisfactory. In particular, the behavior is not customizable to fit your needs. Ultimately, the HTML element <table> is not always what you need. Complex tables with many columns, as those in Figure 4-17, cannot condense as necessary.

Code	Company	Price	Change	In %	Opening	Max	Min	Volume
MSC	Microsoft	$1.38	-0.01	-0.36%	$1.39	$1.39	$1.38	9,395
APP	Apple	$1.99	-0.03	-0.45%	$1.88	$2.15	$1.38	7,741

Figure 4-17. *A full-width table*

But the same table could be changed into a list that could be fully responsive, as shown in Figure 4-18.

Code	MSC
Company	Microsoft
Price	$1.38
Change	-0.01
In %	-0.36%
Opening	$1.39
Max	$1.39
Min	$1.38
Volume	9,395
Code	APP
Company	Apple
Price	$1.99
Change	-0.03
In %	-0.45%
Opening	$1.88
Max	$2.15
Min	$1.38
Volume	7,741

Figure 4-18. *A table at narrow width*

By now many commercial and free grid components produce their presentations with tables. It is often not possible and involves considerable effort to adapt Bootstrap to these constructs. Fortunately, with CSS3 the tables can be adapted. When that does not work, the next step is HTML 5. JavaScript has additional tweaks for even smoother tables. Listing 4-5 takes the code of the table from Figures 4-14 and 4-15:

Listing 4-5. Very Responsive Table with CSS3 (html)

```
1    <table class="table" id="notable">
2    <thead>
3    <tr>
4      <th>Code</th>
5      <th>Company</th>
6      <th>Price</th>
7      <th>Change</th>
8      <th>In %</th>
9      <th>Opening</th>
10     <th>Highest</th>
11     <th>Lowest</th>
12     <th>Volume</th>
13    </tr>
14    </thead>
15    <tbody>
16    <tr>
17      <td data-title="Code">MSF</td>
18      <td data-title="Company">Microsoft</td>
19      <td data-title="Price">$51.38</td>
20      <td data-title="Change">-0.01</td>
21      <td data-title="In %">-0.36%</td>
22      <td data-title="Opening">$51.39</td>
23      <td data-title="Highest">$51.39</td>
24      <td data-title="Lowest">$51.38</td>
```

```
25    <td data-title="Volumen">9,395</td>
26  </tr>
27  <tr>
28    <td data-title="Code">APC</td>
29    <td data-title="Company">Apple</td>
30    <td data-title="Price">$95.46</td>
31    <td data-title="Change">-0.03</td>
32    <td data-title="In %">-0.45%</td>
33    <td data-title="Opening">$91.88</td>
34    <td data-title="Highest">$99.15</td>
35    <td data-title="Lowest">$91.38</td>
36    <td data-title="Volume">7,741</td>
37  </tr>
38  </tbody>
39  </table>
```

The matching CSS looks like Listing 4-6. It is effective only through the @mediaelement, when the screen width falls below 768 px.

Listing 4-6. Very Responsive Table with CSS3 (css)

```
1   @media only screen and (max-width: 768px) {
2
3   /* Prevents the default behavior of a table */
4   #notable table,
5   #notable thead,
6   #notable tbody,
7   #notable th,
8   #notable td,
9   #notable tr {
10  display: block;
11  }
12
```

```
13    /* Hide header */
14    #notable thead tr {
15    position: absolute;
16    top: -9999px;
17    left: -9999px;
18    }
19
20    #notable tr {
21      border: 1px solid #ccc;
22    }
23
24    #notable td {
25    /* Behavior of a number e */
26      border: none;
27      border-bottom: 1px solid #eee;
28      position: relative;
29      padding-left: 50%;
30      white-space: normal;
31      text-align: left;
32    }
33
34    #notable td:before {
35    /* New header */
36      position: absolute;
37    /* Simulation of the distances */
38      top: 6px;
39      left: 6px;
40      width: 145%;
41      padding-right: 10px;
42      white-space: nowrap;
43      text-align: left;
44      font-weight: bold;
```

```
45   /* Get headlines from data-title="" */
46      content: attr(data-title);
47   }
48
49   }
```

The only additional expense is the repetitive usage of attributes to determine the labels with data-title="". Alternatively, you can (with jQuery) use JavaScript so that the header fields get copied automatically.

```
1    $(function () {
2      var t = [];
3      $('thead th').each(function () {
4        t.push($(this).text());
5      });
6      $('tbody tr').each(function() {
7        $(this).find('td').each(function(i, e) {
8          $(e).attr('data-title', t[i]);
9        });
10     });
11   });
```

The script checks for the header fields and creates an array (line 4). Then, it searches for the rows (line 6) and in each row the data-attribute of each element of the array is filled in (line 8).

The repeated declaration of data-title="Code" is no longer necessary and can be removed completely.

No Bootstrap   The path shown in this section supplements the procedure in Bootstrap, but it is largely independent. The basic design and the distances were, however, taken from Bootstrap. You can use the scripting part without Bootstrap and add styles as needed.

Auxiliary Classes

Bootstrap includes a number of helper classes for general purposes.

Spacing Classes

With the containers and the default behavior of the elements, the distances are usually set correctly. However, the result may not correspond to either your design or your aesthetic sensibilities. Even with the use of external components—Bootstrap covers all kinds of elements—there are occasionally unfortunate distances. For this case, there are correction classes. If it is unavoidable, a static rule applies a margin by using

```
1    margin-top: 25px
```

The peculiarity of the distance classes is in the relation to the base font size 1rem. The data are therefore relative.

The structure of the classes is very systematic:

```
1    {Property}{Side}-{Size}
```

Of course, if it matters, you can add the common breakpoint infixes:

```
1    {Property}{Side}-{Breakpoint}-{Size}
```

The property accepts the following values.

- *m*: margin, the distance to the next element.

- *p*: padding, the inner distance of the contents of the element frame.

The side is shown as follows:

- *t*: set the property margin-top or padding-top.

- *b*: set the property margin-bottom or padding-bottom.

- *l*: set the property margin-left or padding-left.

- *r*: set the property margin-right or padding-right.

- *x*: set the property for *-left (left side) and *-right (right side).

- *y*: set the property for *-top (above) and *-bottom (below).

The size is defined as one of these values:

- *auto*: sets the property of all margin or padding rules for all four sides. The size will be determined as follows:

- *0*: Sets all values to 0—no spaces

- *1*: The smallest, *$spacer * 0.25*

- *2*: *$spacer * 0.5*

- *3*: The *$spacer*'s variable default value

- *4*: *$spacer * 1.5*

- *5*: *$spacer * 3*

The value "5" is an especially huge jump compared to other variants.

```
1  .mt-0 {
2    margin-top: 0 !important;
3  }
4
5  .ml-1 {
6    margin-left: $spacer-x !important;
7  }
8
```

```
 9   .px-2 {
10      padding-left: ($spacer-x * 1.5) !important;
11      padding-right: ($spacer-x * 1.5) !important;
12   }
13
14   .pt-auto-3 {
15      padding: ($spacer-y * 3) ($spacer-x * 3) !important;
16   }
```

The variables *$spacer-x* and *$spacer-y* are standard distance.

A special feature is the class *.mx-auto*, which sets the horizontal distance to *auto*, effectively centering an element horizontally.

Negative Margins

For padding values there is no negative option, but for margins it is possible to assign a negative value. It's a common way to move content outside of the natural borders of an element. All the margin classes starting with *.m* accept negative numbers for the size, using the literal "n." This is what the definition looks like:

```
1   .mt-n1 {
2      margin-top: -0.25rem !important;
3   }
```

Sizing Classes

The width and height of elements is usually a pretty simple thing. However, in a grid system the ability to add additional width values is somewhat limited, because values outside the natural grid would lead to elements aligned outside the grid's boundaries. To reduce the risk, some basic width definitions are provided that follow a percentage pattern that aligns better with the grid. See the following example:

```
1   <div class="w-25 p-3">Width 25%</div>
2   <div class="w-50 p-3">Width 50%</div>
3   <div class="w-75 p-3">Width 75%</div>
4   <div class="w-100 p-3">Width 100%</div>
5   <div class="w-auto p-3">Width auto</div>
```

The same pattern is available for vertical measures—simply replace the "w" with "h" (for "height"). Be aware that the browser usually fills the horizontal space usually (100%), because the container element has a definition for this. The height, in contrast, follows the content. To allow the browser to take the whole vertical space you need to add a common definition to your main style sheet like this:

```
1   <style>
2       html, body {
3           height: 100%;
4           margin: 0px;
5       }
6       .container {
7           height: 100%;
8       }
9   </style>
```

This might have an impact on styles for header or footer parts. Carefully test all usage scenarios before relying on the full height definition.

Shadows

If you're not satisfied with alert boxes or cards (explained later in the book), a simple shadow might fit your needs. This is how it can be used:

```
1  <div class="shadow-none p-3 bg-black rounded">No shadow</div>
2  <div class="shadow-sm p-3 bg-white rounded">Small shadow</div>
3  <div class="shadow p-3 bg-white rounded">Regular shadow</div>
4  <div class="shadow-lg p-3 bg-white rounded">Larger shadow</
   div>
```

The suffixes "sm" and "lg" refer to the size of the shadow, not the breakpoints. The shadows are traditionally aligned with the virtual light source in the upper left corner. Hence, the shadow is bigger on the right and bottom border. Be aware that the shadow adds additional space to the content area. If the next element comes quite close, this might need additional space or margin room. In that case, use the auxiliary classes shown in the preceding list.

Stretched Link

A stretched link is a special class that expands the clickable area of a hyperlink to the link's container.

```
1  <div class="w-50 h-50">
2    <a href="#" class="btn btn-secondary stretched-link">
     Go</a>
3  </div>
```

The interesting part here is that the element itself does not appear bigger; only the clickable area grows. The button in the example remains small (following the content), while the container element will fill 50% of the available space.

Be warned that this could be irritating for users, but also quite convenient, depending on where you use it. Test carefully and let some common users give it a try before you officially release your app.

Simple Classes

Some classes replace the common CSS. For example, the `style="position:static"` instruction could be written as `class="position-static."` This applies to all position parameters. The intention is not to save you typing work (it is exactly the same number of characters). The reason is that the definitions can handle different behaviors of browser engines and allow refinements for other classes that need particular values. So even if there is absolutely no visible effect, it is strongly recommended to use such auxiliary classes instead of basic CSS or your own definitions.

The same goes for *.fixed-top* and *.fixed-bottom*, which are also quite simple. They fix an element and prevent it from scrolling with the whole page. If you want an element to scroll but also to stick if the element reaches the border (that is, with the next scroll step it would disappear), the class *.sticky-top* is your solution.

Summary

This chapter covered the basic aspects of typography in Bootstrap. While it is not difficult to use, an application's fonts and styling have a tremendous effect on the overall appearance, look, and feel. The auxiliary classes are a common way to avoid using slightly different styles to apply minor corrections here and there. They make the basic styles themeable, which is important in real-life projects.

CHAPTER 5

Forms

Forms are fully supported in Bootstrap 4. Many of the components are primarily used to make the forms responsive, and can be used with any screen width.

Structure of a Form

Form elements automatically receive the correct formatting. The main class for controls is *.form-control*. Elements that have controllable horizontal extensions such as <input>, <textarea>, and <select> are set to a width of 100% of the parent container. The labels and inputs are grouped using *.formgroup*. They arrange themselves depending on the available width, either side-by-side or one above the other.

Simple Form Elements

Listing 5-1 gives an example of a typical form:

Listing 5-1. Standard Structure of a Form (Form_Base.html)

```
1    <form>
2      <div class="form-group">
3        <label for="txtMail">eMail</label>
4        <input type="email" class="form-control"
5               id="txtMail" placeholder="eMail">
6      </div>
```

```
7      <div class="form-group">
8        <label for="txtPassword">password</label>
9        <input type="password" class="form-control"
10             id="txtPassword" placeholder="Password">
11     </div>
12     <div class="form-group">
13       <label for="txtFile">File Selection</label>
14       <input type="file" class="form-control-file"
         id="txtFile">
15       <p class="form-text small">
16         This is help for upload.
17       </p>
18     </div>
19     <div class="form-check">
20       <input type="checkbox" class="form-check-input"
         id="check">
21       <label class="form-check-label"
         for="check">Save</label>
22     </div>
23     <button type="submit" class="btn btn-secondary">
24       Send
25     </button>
26   </form>
```

The outer section is always the element group *.form-group*. The element is given the *.form-control* class. The other parts do not require explicit classes. Figure 5-1 shows an example of a simple form.

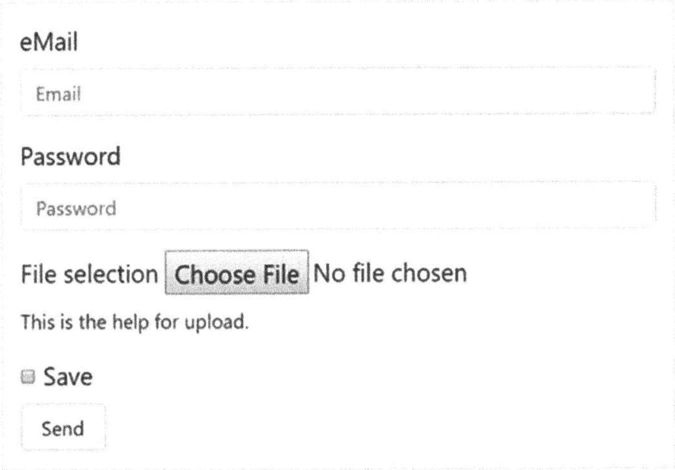

Figure 5-1. *A simple form*

Tip In addition to simple elements, more complex elements can be built out of simpler ones and then put together. This is then referred to as an input group. Element groups and group entries may not be used in mixed input groups, but instead should be nested as a child element.

Single-Line Forms

Single-line forms are available from a width of 768 px and up. "One-line" means that the field name (label), box, and other elements are able to stand side by side, as long as the horizontal space is sufficient. They are preceded by *.form-inline*. Listing 5-2 is a compact form. The enclosing <form> tag is optional. It may be required by the logic of the page or the browser behavior; it does not make a difference to Bootstrap. The width of the elements with variable expansion is "auto." Therefore, the width is optimized within the enclosing container. Sometimes it may be necessary to control the width individually. Figure 5-2 shows a form with horizontal orientation.

Listing 5-2. Compact Form (Form_Inline.html)

```
1    <form class="form-inline">
2      <div class="form-group">
3        <label for="exampleInputName2">Name</label>
4        <input type="text"
5               class="form-control"
6               id="exampleInputName2"
7               placeholder="The Name">
8      </div>
9      <div class="form-group">
10       <label for="exampleInputEmail2">Email</label>
11       <input type="email"
12              class="form-control"
13              id="exampleInputEmail2"
14              placeholder="name@email.com">
15     </div>
16     <div class="form-group">
17       <button type="submit" class="btn btn-secondary float-
         md-right">
18         Send
19       </button>
20     </div>
21   </form>
```

| Name | The Name | eMail | name@email.com |
| | | | Send |

Figure 5-2. *A form with a horizontal orientation (wide)*

Figure 5-3 shows the same form at low screen width.

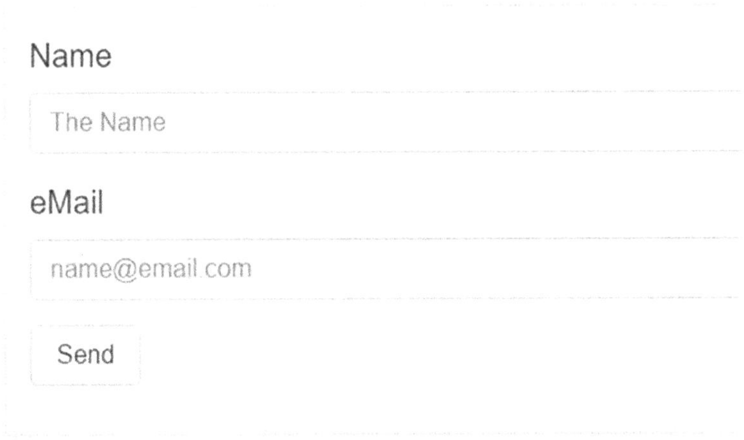

Name

The Name

eMail

name@email.com

Send

Figure 5-3. *A form with a horizontal orientation (narrow)*

Using Labels   You should always use labels, even with one-line forms. Otherwise, screen readers cannot produce meaningful speech. Use *.sr-only* so the label will not appear on regular output devices. If an accessible output is required, the standard attributes `aria-label` or `aria-labelledby` should be used. While aria-label contains the text directly, it is referenced by `arialabelledby="id"` to the ID of another element on the page, which provides the label text.

Listing 5-3 shows the use of invisible text labels. For ordinary users, the watermark (placeholder) is used; however, on other screen readers, the label can be seen. Figure 5-4 shows the form without the label.

Listing 5-3. Form with Watermarks and Screen Readers

```
1    <form class="form-inline">
2      <div class="form-group">
3       <label class="sr-only" for="exampleInputEmail">
4         E-Mail
5       </label>
6       <input type="email" class="form-control"
7               id="exampleInputEmail" placeholder="Email">
8      </div>
9      <div class="form-group">
10       <label class="sr-only" for="exampleInputPassword">
11         Password
12       </label>
13       <input type="password" class="form-control"
14               id="exampleInputPassword"
                placeholder="Password">
15     </div>
16     <div class="form-group form-check">
17       <input type="checkbox" class="form-check-input">
18       <label class="form-check-label sr-only"> Remember</label>
19     </div>
20     <button type="submit" class="btn btn-secondary">
21       Logon
22     </button>
23   </form>
```

Figure 5-4. *A form without label*

Form Elements with Blocks

Input fields, especially those for text entry, can be supplemented for left or right text, icons, or buttons. This is particularly interesting when the values have units. Use the class *.input-group* with *.input-group-append* or *.input-group-prepend* to display elements before or after, using *.formcontrol* to create it. This works very well with all the <input>-elements and with limited success with <select>, but not with <textarea>.

Tooltips and overlapping effects also require additional effort, at least when using the optional *container: "body"* in JavaScript is required to avoid side effects. This parameter determines where the dynamic element in the DOM (document object model) of the page will be inserted.

```
1    $("#toolbarBtn1").dropdown({
2    container: 'body'
3    });
```

The columns of the grid classes cannot mix with the input groups. Instead, the entire input group should be placed in a container if they are required, which in turn is provided with pitches.

Labels are always useful. Even if there is no need for a specific layout, screen readers are supported. In Listing 5-4 and Figure 5-5 the use of *.sr-only* is reattached to achieve this.

Listing 5-4. Fields (Toolbar_Inputgroups.html)

```
1    <div class="input-group">
2        <div class="input-group-prepend">
3            <span class="input-group-text" id="basic-addon1">
             @</span>
4        </div>
5        <input type="text" class="form-control"
         placeholder="User" />
6    </div>
```

```
7
8   <div class="input-group">
9     <input type="text" class="form-control"
      placeholder="Email" />
10      <div class="input-group-append">
11        <span class="input-group-text" id="basic-addon2">
12            @example.de
13        </span>
14      </div>
15  </div>
16
17  <div class="input-group">
18    <div class="input-group-prepend">
19      <span class="input-group-text">&euro;</span>
20    </div>
21    <input type="text" class="form-control" aria-
      label="Amount (in EUR)" />
22    <div class="input-group-append">
23      <span class="input-group-text">.00</span>
24    </div>
25  </div>
```

Figure 5-5. *Fields*

Sizes

Variable sizes can be set relative to the usual four stages. This happens to the entire group, so that individual fields do not always have to be equipped with the class. Listing 5-5 and Figure 5-6 shows the sizes of the input fields.

Listing 5-5. Sizes of the Input Fields (Toolbar_InputSize.html)

```
1    <div class="input-group input-group-lg">
2      <div class="input-group-prepend">
3        <span class="input-group-text" id="sizing-addon1">
         @</span>
4      </div>
5      <input type="text" class="form-control form-control-lg"
       placeholder="Username"/>
6    </div>
7
8    <div class="input-group">
9      <div class="input-group-prepend">
10       <span class="input-group-text" id="sizing-addon2">
         @</span>
11     </div>
12     <input type="text" class="form-control"
       placeholder="Username" />
13   </div>
14
15   <div class="input-group input-group-sm">
16     <div class="input-group-prepend">
17       <span class="input-group-text" id="sizing-addon3">
         @</span>
18     </div>
19     <input type="text" class="form-control form-control-sm"
       placeholder="Username" />
20   </div>
```

Figure 5-6. *Sizes of the input fields*

Dealing with Checkboxes and Radio Buttons

Checkboxes and radio buttons must be placed immediately next to input fields. Groups are used to force the mapping, as shown in Listing 5-6.

Listing 5-6. Fields with Options (Toolbar_Inputradio.html)

```
1    <div class="row">
2      <div class="col-lg-6">
3        <div class="input-group">
4          <div class="input-group-prepend">
5            <span class="input-group-text">
6              <input type="checkbox" aria-label="" />
7            </span>
8          </div>
9          <input type="text" class="form-control" aria-
               label="" />
10       </div>
11     </div>
12     <div class="col-lg-6">
13       <div class="input-group">
14         <div class="input-group-prepend">
15           <span class="input-group-text">
16             <input type="radio" aria-label="" />
17           </span>
```

```
18        </div>
19        <input type="text" class="form-control" aria-
          label="" />
20        </div>
21     </div>
22  </div>
```

To have a useful function, JavaScript is absolutely necessary here—for example, to activate the input box as seen in Figure 5-7.

Figure 5-7. *Input fields with options*

Additional Buttons

Buttons in box groups are treated the same way. They require another nesting of HTML elements based on the class *.input-group-btn*, which is shown in Listing 5-7 and Figure 5-8.

Listing 5-7. Fields with Buttons (Toolbar_InputBtn.html)

```
1   <div class="row">
2     <div class="col-lg-6">
3       <div class="input-group">
4         <span class="input-group-prepend">
5           <button class="btn btn-secondary" type="button">
6             Go!
7           </button>
8         </span>
9         <input type="text" class="form-control"
          placeholder="Search for ..." />
```

```
10        </div>
11      </div>
12      <div class="col-lg-6">
13        <div class="input-group">
14          <input type="text" class="form-control"
            placeholder="Search for..." />
15          <span class="input-group-append">
16            <button class="btn btn-secondary" type="button">
17              Go!
18            </button>
19          </span>
20        </div>
21      </div>
22    </div>
```

Figure 5-8. *Input fields with buttons*

The buttons in turn can be provided with pop-up menus, as illustrated in Listing 5-8 and Figure 5-9.

Listing 5-8. Fields with Menus (Toolbar_DropDownGroup.html)

```
1    <div class="row">
2      <div class="col-lg-6">
3        <div class="input-group">
4          <div class="input-group-prepend">
5            <button type="button"
6                    class="btn btn-secondary dropdown-toggle"
7                    data-toggle="dropdown"
```

```
8              aria-haspopup="true" aria-
               expanded="false">
9          Selection
10        </button>
11        <div class="dropdown-menu">
12          <a class="dropdown-item" href="#">Detail</a>
13          <a class="dropdown-item" href="#">Copy</a>
14          <a class="dropdown-item" href="#">Move</a>
15          <div role="separator" class="dropdown-
               divider"></div>
16          <a class="dropdown-item" href="#">Delete</a>
17        </div>
18      </div>
19      <input type="text" class="form-control" aria-
          label="...">
20    </div>
21  </div>
22  <div class="col-lg-6">
23    <div class="input-group">
24      <input type="text" class="form-control" aria-
          label="...">
25      <div class="input-group-append">
26        <button type="button"
27                class="btn btn-secondary dropdown-toggle"
28                data-toggle="dropdown"
29                aria-haspopup="true" aria-
                  expanded="false">
30          Selection
31        </button>
```

```
32              <div class="dropdown-menu dropdown-menu-right">
33                <a class="dropdown-item" href="#">Detail</a>
34                <a class="dropdown-item" href="#">Copy</a>
35                <a class="dropdown-item" href="#">Move</a>
36                <div role="separator" class="dropdown-
                  divider"></div>
37                <a class="dropdown-item" href="#">Delete</a>
38              </div>
39            </div>
40          </div>
41        </div>
42      </div>
```

Figure 5-9. *Input fields with menus*

Likewise, dividing buttons into segments is possible, as shown in Listing 5-9 and Figure 5-10.

Listing 5-9. Fields with Segment Buttons (Toolbar_InputBtnForm. html)

```
1  <div class="input-group">
2    <div class="input-group-btn">
3      <button class="btn btn-success">Enable</button>
4    </div>
```

142

```
5    <input type="text" class="form-control" aria-
     label="...">
6    </div>
7
8    <div class="input-group">
9      <input type="text" class="form-control" aria-label="..." />
10     <div class="input-group-btn">
11       <button class="btn btn-warning">Disable</button>
12     </div>
13   </div>
```

Figure 5-10. *Input fields with segment buttons*

Listing 5-10 provides a form element that consists of three components: a Euro symbol, the box, and the characters ".00" as a predefined fractional part.

Listing 5-10. Form with Functional Blocks (Form_MultiInput.html)

```
1    <form class="form-inline">
2      <div class="form-group">
3        <label class="sr-only" for="exampleInputAmount">
         Amount (in USD)</label>
4          <div class="input-group">
5            <div class="input-group-prepend">
6              <span class="input-group-text">$</span>
7            </div>
```

```
8              <input type="text" class="form-control"
9                     id="exampleInputAmount"
                      placeholder="Amount">
10             <div class="input-group-append">
11                 <span class="input-group-text">.00</span>
12             </div>
13         </div>
14     </div>
15     <button type="submit" class="btn btn-primary">Wire
       </button>
16   </form>
```

Here the class *.input-group* is used. The label (lines 3 to 5) appears only on screen readers, but otherwise remains invisible. Figure 5-11 shows the form with no label. The "extras" before and after the element are to be decorated with *.input-group-addon*.

Figure 5-11. *A form with no label*

Horizontal Forms

To place labels and fields, a grid is used so that breaks are suppressed. The complete sections of label from one group are normally separated from another using *.formhorizontal* (see Listing 5-11). The particular class is carried in a container element, with either the enclosing <form> element or an equivalent <div> employed. The class *.row* within this container is not necessary. The required grouping *.form-groups* means that the group behaves like one element. You can use *.row*, but some editors complain about it as visible effects are not achieved.

Listing 5-11. Horizontal Form (Form_Horizontal.html)

```
1    <form>
2        <div class="form-group row">
3            <label for="inputEmail3" class="col-2 form-control-
             label">eMail</label>
4            <input type="email" class="form-control col-4"
             id="inputEmail3"
5                    placeholder="E-Mail" />
6            <label for="inputPassword3" class="col-2 form-
             control-label">Password</label>
7            <input type="password" class="form-control col-4"
8                    id="inputPassword3" placeholder="Password" />
9        </div>
10       <div class="form-group row">
11           <div class="offset-2 col-4">
12               <div class="checkbox">
13                   <label> <input type="checkbox" /> Remember
                     </label>
14               </div>
15           </div>
16           <div class="offset-4">
17               <button type="submit" class="btn btn-
                 secondary">Logon</button>
18           </div>
19       </div>
20   </form>
```

In Figure 5-12 the labels are to the left of the elements. When you are working with layouts with narrow widths (in the figure the width is > 768 px), you must go back to the previously shown scheme about placed labels.

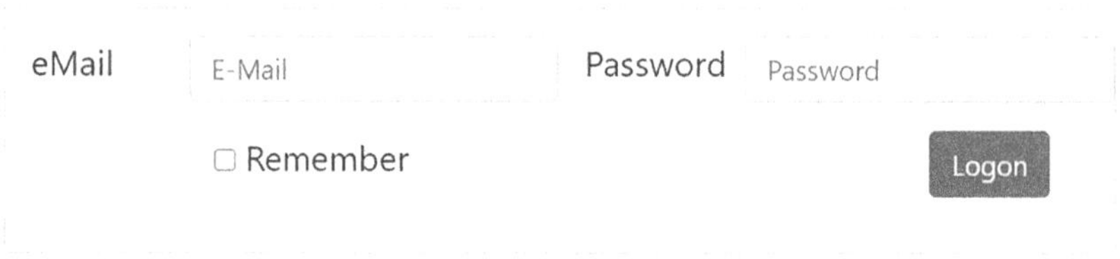

eMail	E-Mail	Password	Password
	☐ Remember		Logon

Figure 5-12. *A form with a label next to the field*

Input Elements

Form elements of the group <input> require the type-attribute to appear properly. They support virtually all the following features of HTML5 types:

- text
- password
- datetime
- datetime-local
- date
- month
- time
- week
- number
- email
- url
- search
- tel
- color

Input Element Syntax

The basic syntax of an input element is shown in the following example.
It can be modified in appearance and behavior by various attributes.
Bootstrap adds additional styling and effects.

```
1    <input type="text"
2            class="form-control"
3            placeholder="Text input">
```

Text fields—that is, multiline edit boxes—drop out of this scheme:

```
1    <textarea class="form-control" rows="3" cols="55"></textarea>
```

Checkboxes and radio buttons function as in the standard
HTML. Locking of an element is also supported with the attribute
disabled. Lock itself works not only with the control, but also relates to the
associated label using the class *.disabled*. This class is also associated with
.radio, .radio-inline, .checkbox, .checkbox-inline, or <fieldset>. They can
be used as in Listing 5-12 to format the enclosing container.

Listing 5-12. Checkboxes and Radio Buttons (Form_Elements.html)

```
1    <form>
2      <div class="form-check">
3        <input class="form-check-input" type="checkbox"
         value="" />
4        <label class="form-check-label"> Option one </label>
5      </div>
6      <div class="form-check">
7        <input class="form-check-input" type="checkbox"
         value="" disabled />
8        <label class="form-check-label"> Option two
         (deactivated) </label>
9      </div>
```

```
10     <div class="form-check">
11       <input class="form-check-input" type="radio"
         name="optionsRadios"
12             id="optionsRadios1" value="option1" checked />
13       <label class="form-check-label"> Option one </label>
14     </div>
15     <div class="form-check">
16       <input class="form-check-input" type="radio"
         name="optionsRadios"
17             id="optionsRadios2" value="option2" />
18       <label class="form-check-label"> Option two </label>
19     </div>
20     <div class="form-check">
21       <input class="form-check-input" type="radio"
         name="optionsRadios"
22             id="optionsRadios3" value="option3" disabled />
23       <label class="form-check-label"> Option three </label>
24     </div>
25   </form>
```

The <label> element enclosing the radio button or checkbox is shown here in Figure 5-13. In this way a single click triggers the label text from the action, resulting in a more pleasant user experience.

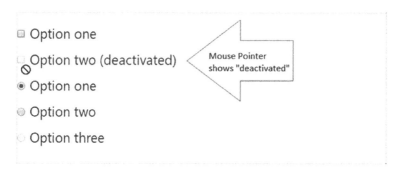

Figure 5-13. *Checkboxes and radio buttons*

The classes *.checkbox-inline* or *.radio-inline* allow a string of elements next to each other (see Listing 5-13 and Figure 5-14).

Listing 5-13. Checkboxes and Radio Buttons Next to Each Other (Form_ElementsHor. html)

```
1   <form>
2     <div class="form-check form-check-inline">
3       <input class="form-check-input"  type="checkbox"
4               id="inlineCheckbox1" value="option1" />
5       <label class="form-check-label"
        for="inlineCheckbox1">1</label>
6     </div>
7     <div class="form-check form-check-inline">
8       <input class="form-check-input"  type="checkbox"
9               id="inlineCheckbox2" value="option2" />
10      <label class="form-check-label"
        for="inlineCheckbox2">2</label>
11    </div>
12    <div class="form-check form-check-inline">
13      <input class="form-check-input"  type="checkbox"
14              id="inlineCheckbox3" value="option3" />
15      <label class="form-check-label"
        for="inlineCheckbox3">3</label>
16    </div>
17    <div class="form-check form-check-inline">
18      <input class="form-check-input"  type="radio"
        name="inlineRadioOptions"
19              id="inlineRadio1" value="option1" />
20      <label class="form-check-label" for="inlineRadio1">1
        </label>
21    </div>
```

```
22    <div class="form-check form-check-inline">
23      <input class="form-check-input"  type="radio"
        name="inlineRadioOptions"
24            id="inlineRadio2" value="option2" />
25      <label class="form-check-label" for="inlineRadio2">2
        </label>
26    </div>
27    <div class="form-check form-check-inline">
28      <input class="form-check-input"  type="radio"
        name="inlineRadioOptions"
29            id="inlineRadio3" value="option3" />
30      <label class="form-check-label" for="inlineRadio3">3
        </label>
31    </div>
32  </form>
```

☐ 1 ☑ 2 ☐ 3 ○ 1 ◉ 2 ○ 3

Figure 5-14. *Checkboxes and radio buttons next to each other*

If default behavior is required but no label text is needed, delete the text and let the label surrounding the box.

```
1  <div class="form-check">
2    <label class="form-check-label">
3      <input class="form-check-input" type="checkbox"
        id="blankCheckbox"
4            value="1" aria-label="...">
5    </label>
6  </div>
7  <div class="form-check">
```

```
 8    <label class="form-check-label">
 9      <input class="form-check-input" type="radio"
        name="blankRadio" id="blankRadio1"
10            value="1" aria-label="...">
11    </label>
12  </div>
```

Select Elements

Lists and drop-down menus can be used as usual. However, some browsers turn to internal styles that cannot be influenced with CSS. It could be that menus are a better choice to get full control over the design.

For simple folding menus, select one of the following options.

```
1  <select class="custom-select">
2    <option>1</option>
3    <option>2</option>
4    <option>3</option>
5    <option>4</option>
6    <option>5</option>
7  </select>
```

With the attribute multiple it is possible to select multiple options.

```
1  <select multiple class="custom-select">
2    <option>1</option>
3    <option>2</option>
4    <option>3</option>
5    <option>4</option>
6    <option>5</option>
7  </select>
```

Static Texts in Forms

Help texts and static blocks are provided with *form-control-static* by a defined section <p>. Listing 5-14 shows static elements in the layout and Figure 5-15 shows the static elements in a horizontal layout. Listing 5-15 shows the display fields (help texts) and Figure 5-16 shows static elements with additional text in horizontal layout.

Listing 5-14. Static Elements in the Layout (Form_Help.html)

```
1   <form class="row">
2      <div class="form-group">
3        <label class="col-2 form-control-label">eMail</label>
4          <div class="col-10">
5            <p class="form-control-static">email@example.
              com</p>
6          </div>
7      </div>
8      <div class="form-group">
9        <label for="inputPassword" class="col-2 form-
          control-label">Password</label>
10         <div class="col-10">
11           <input type="password" class="form-control"
              id="inputPassword"
12                    placeholder="Password" />
13         </div>
14     </div>
15  </form>
```

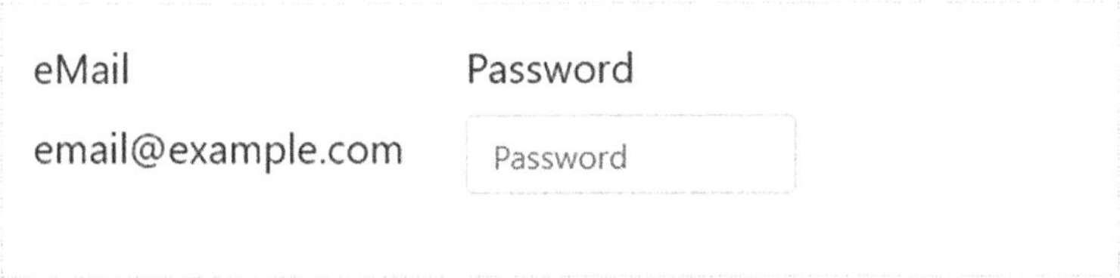

eMail   Password

email@example.com   Password

Figure 5-15. Static elements in horizontal layout

Listing 5-15. Display Fields (Form_HelpInline.html)

```
1    <form class="form-inline">
2      <div class="form-group">
3        <label class="sr-only">eMail</label>
4        <p class="form-control-static">email@example.com</p>
5      </div>
6      <div class="form-group">
7        <label for="inputPassword2" class="sr-only">
8          Password
9        </label>
10       <input type="password" class="form-control"
11              id="inputPassword2" placeholder="Password">
12     </div>
13     <button type="submit" class="btn btn-secondary">
14       Confirm
15     </button>
16   </form>
```

email@example.com   Password   Confirm

Figure 5-16. Static text in a form with horizontal layout

Behavior of the Form Elements

Form elements respond dynamically to the focus. The frame is removed and when obtaining the focus a soft shadow appears. Trigger is the pseudoclass *:focus*. Disabled controls use disabled (line 5) and are presented somewhat lighter.

```
1    <input class="form-control"
2           id="disabledInput"
3           type="text"
4           placeholder="Locked content..."
5           disabled>
```

If you use <fieldset> and disabled, you can block several elements together. However, the blocking of the user actions relates only to regular form elements (see Listing 5-16 and Figure 5-17). Hyperlinks are not blocked. If hyperlinks are formatted as buttons (<a ... class="btn btn-*">), however, they act more like links. The desired effect can be done with JavaScript. However, Bootstrap works only with a gray appearance.

Listing 5-16. Locked Fields (Form_Disabled.html)

```
1    <form>
2      <fieldset disabled>
3        <div class="form-group">
4          <label for="disabledTextInput">Disabled Field
           </label>
5          <input type="text" id="disabledTextInput"
6                 class="form-control" placeholder="Disabled
                  field" />
7        </div>
8        <div class="form-group">
9          <label for="disabledSelect">Disabled Menu</label>
```

154

```
10        <select id="disabledSelect" class="custom-select">
11          <option>Option A Disabled</option>
12          <option>Option B Disabled</option>
13        </select>
14      </div>
15      <div class="form-check">
16        <input type="checkbox" class="form-check-input" />
17        <label class="form-check-label">Checkbox</label>
18      </div>
19      <button type="submit" class="btn btn-primary">Send
          </button>
20    </fieldset>
21  </form>
```

Disabled Field

Disabled field

Disabled Menu

Option A Disabled

Checkbox

Send

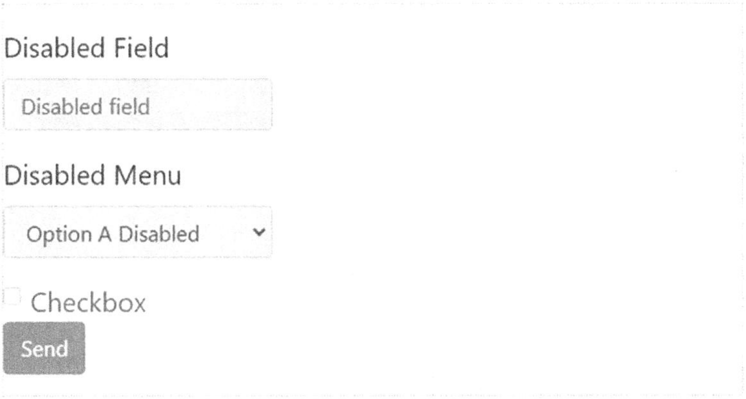

Figure 5-17. *Locked elements (with mouse)*

In addition to blocking or lock elements, you can use a similar condition for read-only. This is based on the HTML attribute readonly. The element is lighter and therefore at first looks like disabled; however, the pointer remains unchanged and does not show the lock icon (see Listing 5-17).

155

Listing 5-17. Read-Only Mode (Excerpt from Form_ReadOnly.html)

```
1   <input class="form-control" type="text"
2           placeholder="Read Only..."
3           readonly>
```

In particular, the behavior of drop-down lists is different. Unlike disabled, the user can select from the elements and view them. A selection of data when sending the readonly form still does not succeed. Figure 5-18 shows a read-only form.

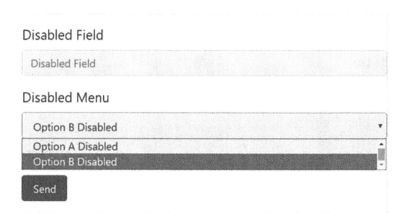

Figure 5-18. *Elements in read-only mode*

Validation Information in Forms

Bootstrap supports HTML 5 validation states. These are represented by the HTML 5 pseudoclasses such as *:invalid* or *:valid*. If it is not possible to use these for some reason, a fallback is available using the regular classes *.is-invalid* and *.is-valid*. The limitation to just two states, valid and invalid, is different from Bootstrap 3, where a third state, "warning" was available. If you need such states, use regular form elements with icons and semantic classes.

Elements that have either of the classes *.form-control* or *.form-text* can be modified to match their status (see Listing 5-18 and Figure 5-19).

Accessibility   The status shows with a color. Colorblind users may not benefit from this information. Therefore, the semantic meaning should always accompany the color information. This can be achieved by help texts, symbols, and *.sr-only* regions. elements that cannot be adapted should carry an aria-invalid="true" attribute. Accessibility is handled widely by the ARIA standard (Accessible Rich Internet Applications), a W3C working draft published by the Web Applications Working Group. Examples that mention "ARIA" in this chapter refer to the related standardization documents.

Listing 5-18. Semantic Information in the Input Fields (Form_Semantic.html)

```
1    <div class="row">
2      <form class="needs-validation" novalidate>
3        <div class="form-group">
4          <label for="input1">
5            Success message
6          </label>
7          <input type="text" class="form-control is-valid"
             id="input1" required />
8          <div class="valid-feedback text-success">Ok</div>
9        </div>
10       <div class="form-group">
11         <label for="input3">
12           Error condition
13         </label>
```

```
14        <input type="text" class="form-control is-invalid"
          id="input3" required />
15        </div>
16        <div class="form-check">
17            <input type="checkbox"  class="form-check-input
              is-valid" id="checkboxSuccess" value="option1" />
18            <label class="form-check-label">Successful</label>
19          </label>
20        </div>
21        <div class="form-check">
22            <input type="checkbox" class="form-check-input
              is-invalid" id="checkboxError" value="option1"
              required />
23            <label class="form-check-label">
24            Error condition
25          </label>
26        </div>
27        <button class="btn btn-primary" type="submit">Test
          Form</button>
28      </form>
29    </div>)
```

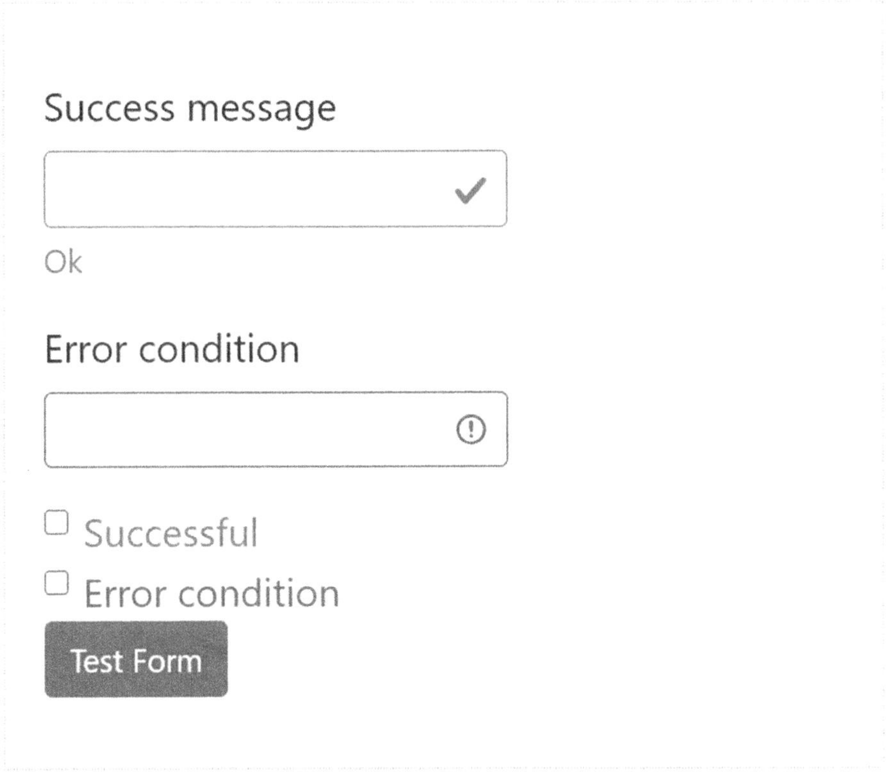

Success message

Ok

Error condition

☐ Successful
☐ Error condition

Test Form

Figure 5-19. *Semantic form elements*

As an option, use states with upgraded symbols. This can be accomplished with *.valid-feedback* or *.invalid-feedback* and a symbol on the right end of the message areas. These icons will only work if <input class="form-control"> is used.

Listing 5-19 shows what a completely accessible form can look like.

Listing 5-19. Semantic and Disability Aware Form (Form_AriaSemantic.html)

```
1     <div class="container">
2       <div class="row">
3         <form class="needs-validation" novalidate>
```

```
4           <div class="form-group">
5             <label for="inputSuccess3">Success Test</label>
6             <input type="text" class="form-control"
              id="inputSuccess3" />
7             <div class="valid-feedback">Success</div>
8           </div>
9           <div class="form-group ">
10            <label for="inputGroupError2">Error Test</label>
11            <div class="input-group">
12              <div class="input-group-prepend">
13                <span class="input-group-text">@</span>
14              </div>
15              <input type="text" class="form-control"
                id="inputGroupError2" required />
16            </div>
17            <div class="invalid-feedback">Error</div>
18          </div>
19          <button class="btn btn-primary"
            type="submit">Test</button>
20        </form>
21      </div>
22    </div>
23    <script>
24      (function() {
25        'use strict';
26        window.addEventListener('load', function() {
27          // Fetch all the forms we want to apply custom
             Bootstrap validation styles to
28          var forms = document.querySelectorAll('.needs-
             validation');
```

```
29          // Loop over them and prevent submission
30          var validation = Array.prototype.filter.
            call(forms, (form) => {
31            form.addEventListener('submit', (event) => {
32              if (form.checkValidity() === false) {
33                event.preventDefault();
34                event.stopPropagation();
35              }
36              form.classList.add('was-validated');
37            }, false);
38          });
39        }, false);
40      })();
41    </script>
```

An additional font library is not required, and the styling shown is the default behavior. The JavaScript in the previous example is just to prevent the browser from reloading the page and invoke the validation process. The effect is shown in Figure 5-20. There is, however, no actual validation, and you must add custom code to have full validation support.

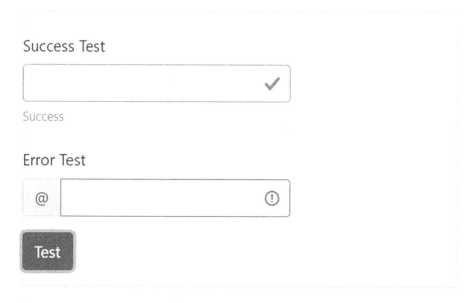

Figure 5-20. *Semantic elements with ARIA support*

Listing 5-20 depicts a form with a success and error message (see Figure 5-21) in a slightly different form. Here we use the tooltip approach that overlays the text.

Listing 5-20. Semantic Messages (Form_Success.html)

```
1    <form class="needs-validation" novalidate>
2      <div class="form-group position-relative">
3          <label for="inputEmail">Email</label>
4          <input type="email" class="form-control is-valid"
           id="inputEmail"
5                  placeholder="Email" value="joerg@krause.net"
                   required>
6          <div class="valid-tooltip">Your email address looks
           good.</div>
7      </div>
```

```
8    <div class="form-group position-relative">
9        <label for="inputPassword">Password</label>
10       <input type="password" class="form-control is-
         invalid" id="inputPassword"
11                placeholder="Password" required>
12       <div class="invalid-tooltip">Password not
         recognized.</div>
13   </div>
14   <button type="submit" class="btn btn-primary">Sign in
     </button>
15   </form>
```

The overlapping tooltip might require additional styling to justify the margins. This is an option if the space is somehow limited and dynamically visible error messages destroy the form's layout.

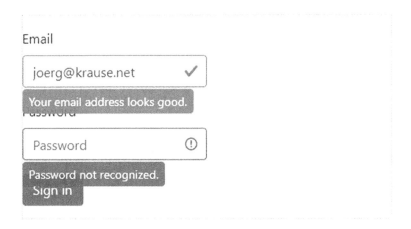

Figure 5-21. Semantic messages

Optional symbols with hidden .sr-only sections support screen readers. The icon is automatically properly aligned, as shown in Listing 5-21.

Listing 5-21. Messages for Screen Readers (Form_SuccessSR.html)

```
1   <form class="needs-validation" novalidate>
2     <div class="form-group position-relative">
3       <label for="inputEmail">Email</label>
4       <input type="email" class="form-control is-valid"
        id="inputEmail" placeholder="Email" value="joerg@
        krause.net" required />
5       <div class="valid-tooltip">Your email address looks
        good.</div>
6       <div class="valid-tooltip sr-only">Success! Email
        address looks good.</div>
7     </div>
8     <div class="form-group position-relative">
9       <label for="inputPassword">Password</label>
10      <input type="password" class="form-control is-invalid"
        id="inputPassword" placeholder="Password" required />
11      <div class="invalid-tooltip">Password not
        recognized.</div>
12      <div class="invalid-tooltip sr-only">Error! Password
        not recognized.</div>
13    </div>
14    <button type="submit" class="btn btn-primary">Sign in</
      button>
15  </form>
```

Form Elements in the Grid

Use the usual techniques when formatting width and height. For the width make use of the grid, with classes such as *.col-3* or *.col-5* (see Listing 5-22 and Figure 5-22). Adjust the setting for specific breakpoints by using the common infix values, such as *.col-md-2* or *.col-lg-5*.

Listing 5-22. Arrangement in the Grid (Form_Grid.html)

```
1    <div class="row">
2      <div class="col-2">
3        <input type="text"
4                class="form-control"
5                placeholder="2 columns">
6      </div>
7      <div class="col-3">
8        <input type="text"
9                class="form-control"
10               placeholder="3 columns">
11     </div>
12     <div class="col-4">
13       <input type="text"
14               class="form-control"
15               placeholder="4 columns">
16     </div>
17   </div>
```

Figure 5-22. *Elements aligned with the grid*

Adaptation of the Field Height

There are two classes for controlling height: *.form-group-sm* and *.form-group-lg* (see Listing 5-23 and Figure 5-23).

165

Listing 5-23. Size of the Elements (Form_ElementsSize.html)<form>

```
1      <div class="form-group">
2         <input class="form-control form-control-lg"
3                type="text" placeholder="Big">
4      </div>
5      <div class="form-group">
6         <input class="form-control"
7                type="text" placeholder="Normal">
8      </div>
9      <div class="form-group">
10        <input class="form-control form-control-sm"
11               type="text" placeholder="Small">
12     </div>
13     <div class="form-group">
14        <select class="custom-select form-control-lg">
15           <option>1</option>
16           <option>2</option>
17           <option>3</option>
18        </select>
19     </div>
20     <div class="form-group">
21        <select class="custom-select">
22           <option>1</option>
23           <option>2</option>
24           <option>3</option>
25        </select>
26     </div>
27     <div class="form-group">
28        <select class="custom-select form-control-sm">
29           <option>1</option>
30           <option>2</option>
```

```
31            <option>3</option>
32          </select>
33      </div>
34    </form>
```

Figure 5-23. *Elements in various sizes*

The size of horizontal running forms can be controlled globally. For this purpose, the class *.form-horizontal* can use either class *.form-group-lg* or *.form-group-sm* (see Listing 5-24 and Figure 5-24).

Listing 5-24. Size of the Elements (Form_ElementsSizeHor.html)

```
1    <form>
2      <div class="form-group row">
3        <label class="col-2 form-control-label"
4              for="formGroupInputLarge">Big Label</label>
```

167

```
 5       <div class="col-10">
 6         <input class="form-control form-control-lg"
           type="text"
 7                   id="formGroupInputLarge" placeholder="Big
                     input">
 8       </div>
 9     </div>
10     <div class="form-group row">
11       <label class="col-2 form-control-label small"
12               for="formGroupInputSmall">Small Label</label>
13       <div class="col-10">
14         <input class="form-control form-control-sm"
           type="text"
15                   id="formGroupInputSmall" placeholder="Small
                     input">
16       </div>
17     </div>
18   </form>
```

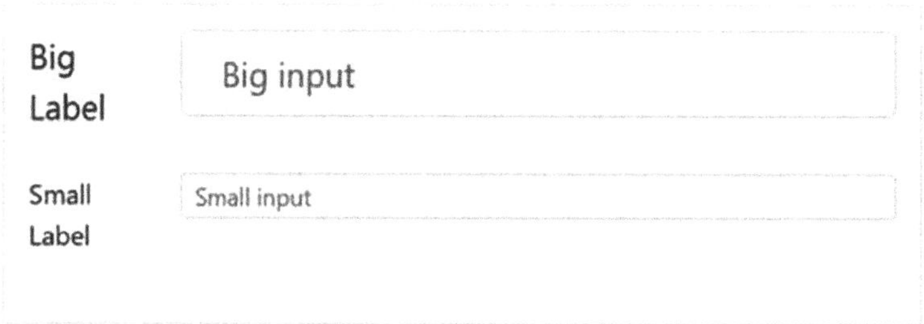

Figure 5-24. *Elements aligned*

Help Text in Forms

Help texts for forms are often needed (see Listing 5-25 and Figure 5-25). There is one for display and one for screen readers to support accessible pages. For these to work, the matching *aria* attributes (attributes that support the ARIA standard start with the prefix "aria-") should always be used with the Bootstrap classes together.

Listing 5-25. Help Text in Forms (Form_ElementsHelp.html)

```
1    <form>
2      <div class="form-group form-group-lg">
3        <label for="inputHelpBlock">Your input</label>
4          <input type="text" id="inputHelpBlock"
             class="form-control"
5            aria-describedby="helpBlock">
6          <span id="helpBlock" class="text-black-50 small">
7            You can enter something here.
8          </span>
9      </div>
10   </form>
```

Use any of the *.text-** classes to style the help text according to your needs.

Your input

You can enter something here.

Figure 5-25. *Help texts*

Buttons

Buttons can be found in one form or another in each web application. Bootstrap buttons are seen as a design element that is separate from the technical framework. Technically, a "submit" appears only once in a form, which almost always triggers a POST request. If, however, you need access to the server via a GET request, a hyperlink is used. In design terms, Bootstrap provides both in the same layout. Button-like elements can be created with <a>, <button>, or <input> (see Listing 5-26 and see Figure 5-26).

Listing 5-26. Button-Like Elements (Excerpt from Form_Buttons. html)

```
1   <a class="btn btn-secondary" href="#" role="button">
2     Link
3   </a>
4   <button class="btn btn-secondary" type="Submit">
5     Button
6   </button>
7   <input class="btn btn-secondary"
8          type="button" value="Input">
9   <input class="btn btn-secondary"
10         type="submit" value="Submit">
```

Figure 5-26. *Buttons—several variants of the same effect*

However, there is one restriction: in navigation bars built with *.nav* or *.navbar*, only the common element <button> is allowed.

If <a> tags are used as a button, they should only serve the navigation and not trigger as a hyperlink, because this is not the expected behavior. Moreover, it should be emphasized by the attribute role="button." Even then it is questionable whether this is a good idea, as not all browsers can ensure that the function will behave as expected. So take advantage of the distinct buttons and whenever possible, it is preferable to use <button>.

Semantic Buttons

Buttons are available in seven variants with the following semantic expressions (see Listing 5-27 and Figure 5-27).

- *Primary*: raises the main function, visual effect by blue color amplified.

- *Secondary*: standard, gray, general function.

- *Success*: success, green, positive, or affirmative action.

- *Info*: information, azure, clarified highlighting critical or special actions.

- *Warning*: warning, orange, critical or complex action, should be taken with caution.

- *Danger*: danger, red, dangerous or irreversible action, negative.

- *Link*: formats a button as a link, often referred to as reduced action, additional behavior.

Listing 5-27. Semantic Buttons (excerpt from Form_Buttons.html)

```
1   <button type="button" class="btn btn-secondary">Secondary
    </button>
2   <button type="button" class="btn btn-
    primary">Primary</button>
```

```
3    <button type="button" class="btn btn-
     success">Succes</button>
4    <button type="button" class="btn btn-info">Info</button>
5
6    <button type="button" class="btn btn-
     warning">Warning</button>
7    <button type="button" class="btn btn-
     danger">Danger</button>
```

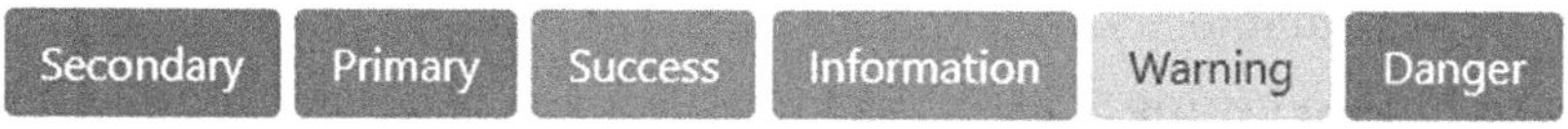

Figure 5-27. *Semantic buttons*

Assigning semantic meanings on the color labels may be restricted by size in some environments. Additional labels, which are equipped with *.sr-only*, should emphasize the intended effect.

Size and Appearance

For the larger or smaller button classes, *.btn-lg* or *.btn-sm* should be used (see Figure 5-28). They complement the base class *btn* and are independent of color. The standard size is ready for touch operation. Mouse-controlled sites will look better with the smaller buttons.

```
1    <form>
2      <button type="button" class="btn btn-primary btn-lg">
       Big</button>
3      <button type="button" class="btn btn-secondary btn-lg">
       Big</button>
4    </form>
5    <form>
```

```
6    <button type="button" class="btn btn-primary">Default
     </button>
7    <button type="button" class="btn btn-
     secondary">Default</button>
8    </form>
9    <form>
10   <button type="button" class="btn btn-primary btn-sm">
     Small</button>
11   <button type="button" class="btn btn-secondary btn-sm">
     Small</button>
12   </form>
```

Figure 5-28. *Size of the buttons*

Sometimes buttons will completely fill their containers. This is the purpose of the class *.btn-block* (see Listing 5-28). To form a complete container, you need a *.row* and a *.col* class enabled element.

Listing 5-28. Buttons Horizontally Extended (Form_ButtonsContainer.html)

```
1    <div class="row">
2      <div class="col">
3        <button type="button" class="btn btn-primary btn-lg
         btn-block">Block</button>
4        <button type="button" class="btn btn-secondary btn-lg
         btn-block">Block</button>
5      </div>
6    </div>
```

Note here that this only affects the width. Appropriate height must be reached separately with *.btn-lg* or other size as necessary (see Figure 5-29).

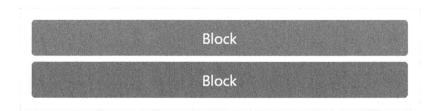

Figure 5-29. *Buttons horizontally expanded*

Displaying outline buttons is new in Bootstrap 4. The visual impact of previous buttons is avoided. So far the elements benefit from a weak gradient, which produces a slight 3D effect. They are often used in newer sites with modern flat, reduced designs that seem overloaded. Listing 5-29 shows you how to grab the "outline" buttons. The result is shown in Figure 5-30.

Listing 5-29. Semantic Buttons with Frame

```
1   <button type="button"
2           class="btn btn-outline-secondary">Secondary</button>
3   <button type="button"
4           class="btn btn-outline-primary">Primary</button>
5   <button type="button"
6           class="btn btn-outline-success">Success</button>
7   <button type="button"
8           class="btn btn-outline-info">Info</button>
9   <button type="button"
10          class="btn btn-outline-warning">Warning</button>
11  <button type="button"
12          class="btn btn-outline-danger">Danger</button>
```

Figure 5-30. *Semantic buttons with frame*

States

The disabled state can be achieved on hyperlinks and on buttons.
Listing 5-30 shows an example for hyperlinks:

Listing 5-30. Set the Active State for Link Buttons

```
1    <a href="#"
2        class="btn btn-primary btn-lg active"
3        role="button">
4      Primary
5    </a>
6    <a href="#"
7        class="btn btn-secondary btn-lg active"
8        role="button">
9      Link
10   </a>
```

The disabled state indicates that the button cannot be pressed. For
this, the HTML attribute disabled is used. Figure 5-31 shows various states
of a button as shown in Listing 5-31.

Listing 5-31. The States for Buttons Use the Same Class

```
1    <form>
2        <button type="button" class="btn btn-primary btn-lg
         active">Primary</button>
3        <button type="button" class="btn btn-secondary btn-lg
         active">Secondary</button>
4        <hr/>
```

```
5       <a href="#" class="btn btn-primary btn-lg active"
        role="button">Primary</a>
6       <a href="#" class="btn btn-secondary btn-lg active"
        role="button">Link</a>
7       <hr />
8       <button type="button" class="btn btn-lg btn-primary"
        disabled="disabled">Primary</button>
9       <button type="button" class="btn btn-secondary btn-lg"
        disabled="disabled">Secondary</button>
10      <hr />
11      <a href="#" class="btn btn-primary btn-lg disabled"
        role="button">Primary</a>
12      <a href="#" class="btn btn-secondary btn-lg disabled"
        role="button">Link</a>
13    </form>
```

If a hyperlink is formatted as a button the class *.disabled* is being used, as shown in Listing 5-32.

Listing 5-32. Disabled Hyperlinks

```
1    <a href="#"
2       class="btn btn-primary btn-lg disabled"
3       role="button">Primary</a>
4    <a href="#"
5       class="btn btn-secondary btn-lg disabled"
6       role="button">Link</a>
```

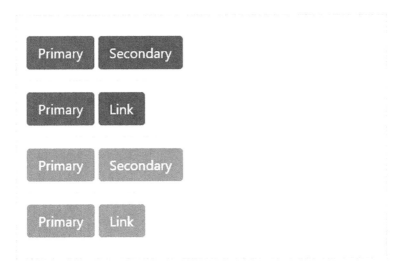

Figure 5-31. *Various states of a button*

Warning   Note that the cut-off of elements with CSS classes is merely cosmetic. This is also the case with pointer-events: even if there are none internally, this does not prevent those elements from being selected with the keyboard, and they can still trigger actions. You need to check with JavaScript that the function will coincide with the presentation.

Summary

This chapter examined the basic ways to style forms. Apart from the default behavior, Bootstrap adds to any form the validation response based on the attributes defined by HTML 5. In this chapter you also got an idea what semantic styling is about and how to use it for fields and buttons.

CHAPTER 6

Images, Effects, and Icons

This chapter is about images, effects, and symbols. The only images supported are some effects that are available here.

Icons

The symbols—font-based icons—are the basis of the icon functions. The glyphs used in Bootstrap 3 are called Halflings (a reference to *Lord of the Rings*) and are usually not free. Bootstrap 4 no longer contains the Glyphicons, and you have to use one of the many font libraries.

Why symbol fonts?   Font-based icons avoid the problem of individual symbols leading to a flood of additional requests on the server. Instead, all the symbols are loaded as a font—that is, in one file. However, the symbol is then like a letter. It is changeable in size and extent, but it may take only one color. Fonts are also mainly flat; 3D effects are eliminated. For fast, modern web sites, so-called glyph fonts are an established technology.

© Jörg Krause 2020
J. Krause, *Introducing Bootstrap 4*, https://doi.org/10.1007/978-1-4842-6203-0_6

Alternatives

The following alternatives are currently available (see Figure 6-1 for a sample of Octicons):

- Font Awesome (`http://fortawesome.github.io/Font-Awesome/`)— number depends on license and package

- Feather (`https://feathericons.com/`)—282 icons (2020)

- Octicons, the Github Icons (`https://octicons.github.com/`)—160 symbols

- Elegant Icon Font (`http://www.elegantthemes.com/blog/resources/elegant-icon-font`)—360 symbols

- Typicons (`http://typicons.com/`–336 symbols

- Meteocons (`http://www.alessioatzeni.com/meteocons`)—40+ weather symbols

- Open Iconic (`https://useiconic.com/open`)—223 symbols, which can be up to 8 px down

This is only a small selection, and provided here to encourage you to seek the right support before your first design experiments. The first three are recommended by Bootstrap, but the decision on which icons to use is up to you. Consider the icon set's style, license (free or paid), and your personal preferences.

Figure 6-1. *The free symbol font Octicons (MIT license from Github, Inc.)*

Use of Symbols

The following example illustrates the procedure using the library *Font Awesome*. You can get the files with npm, for example:

```
1   $ npm install font-awesome
```

The configuration file for npm, package.json, looks like this (excerpt):

```
1     "dependencies": {
2       "bootstrap": "^4.5.0",
3       "font-awesome": "^4.7.0",
4       "jquery": "^3.5.1",
5       "popper.js": "^1.16.1"
6     }
```

In the HTML file another link comes with the CSS definitions:

```
1   <link href="css/font-awesome.css" rel="stylesheet" />
```

The CSS file contains references by URLs to the actual font files. You must add these files to your deployment package. In web sites with static files, that means you copy the font files from *node_modules* to the destination folder. Fonts come usually in different versions to support any number of browsers. However, these days almost all devices support **.woff2* files. It's probably enough to copy just these. Other formats are **.ttf* (TrueType), **.svg* (Scalable Vector Graphics), **.woff*, and **.eot*. While copying too much may not really harm your apps performance, other techniques might suffer. If you use WebPack and pack the files into the bundle, the bundle will increase dramatically in size.

To keep the definition compact, all symbols are based on a base class and a class for the icon, which achieves the effect. Note that the symbol is technically a character. If an icon appears on a button in the text or as an addition of a text, it should be separated by a space.

Icon classes should always be an exclusive item, and you should not divide the element with other classes. When in doubt, add an extra `<span>`-Element. Avoid child elements as well. If symbols have no semantic meaning but merely serve decorative purposes, avoid problems with screen readers with `aria-hidden="true."` Conversely, you should explicitly support screen readers when the symbol has a meaning, and add text hidden with *.sr-only*.

```
<span class="fa fa-search"
aria-hidden="true"></span>
```

Use of Buttons

Listing 6-1 and Figure 6-2 give some examples to show how symbols can be used on buttons. In this example I use Font-Awesome:

Listing 6-1. Buttons with Icons (Icons_Btn.html)

```
<button type="button"
        class="btn btn-secondary"
        aria-label="Left Align">
<span class="fa fa-align-left"
      aria-hidden="true">
</span>
</button>
<button type="button"
        class="btn btn-secondary btn-lg">
<span class="fa fa-star"
      aria-hidden="true">
</span> Star
</button>
```

Figure 6-2. *Buttons with icons*

Messages

In a message, symbols are suitable for highlighting or for an opportunity to dismiss the message (see Listing 6-2 and Figure 6-3).

Listing 6-2. Messages with Symbols (Icons_Messages.html)

```
<div class="alert alert-danger" role="alert">
<span class="fa fa-exclamation"
     aria-hidden="true"></span>
<span class="sr-only">Error</span>
     Please enter a valid address
</div>
```

> **!** Please enter a valid address

Figure 6-3. *Messages with icons*

Common Symbols

You can define an icon that closes dialogs or messages as follows (see Figure 6-4). This is an example of a pure HTML icon, a so-called entity. Today web documents are almost always encoded in UTF-8. This encoding comes with a rich set of symbols. These are not purely icons, but any kind of letters, numbers, and signs for different purposes. This includes arrows, mathematical symbols, letters for different languages such as greek or arabic, and so on. Some of these signs have entity names, such as λ (the Greek letter). Many have just a number, written as Λ (Hex, also Lamda) or Λ (Decimal, also Lamda). Some advice: even if your programming environment (Java, or .NET for example) supports UTF-16 and HTML 5 is compatible with UTF-16, it's common practice to use UTF-8 for web sites. Be aware that Unicode is a character set and UTF-8 is an encoding. An encoding translates numbers into binary representation. Character sets translate characters to numbers.

```
<button type="button" class="close" aria-label="Close">
    Message
<span aria-hidden="true">&times;</span>
</button>
```

Figure 6-4. *Effect of a "close" button (nonfunctional)*

To indicate a context menu, use a *.caret* as shown in Figure 6-5.

```
1    <span class="caret"></span>
```

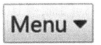

Figure 6-5. *Effect for drop-down menus (nonfunctional)*

Responsive Images

Images typically have natural expansion. On large screens this is not critical, but shown on small devices, they may leave the viewing area. With *.img-fluid* you can present better images.

This class enforces three actions:

- *max-width: 100%*
- *height: Auto*
- *display: Block*

Thus, the image is scaled to the device width and remains stable. Should it be extremely reduced compared to the natural size, you may want to consider scaling with a server-side solution. By not doing so you waste a lot of bandwidth and have little effect on the user.

If *.img-fluid* is used, there are other options available. The class *.center-block* centers the image in the container.

SVG and IE 8 to 10   In Internet Explorer 8 to 10 sVG (scalable vector graphics) images are scaled unfavorably with *.img-fluid*. to solve this, you should add the style rule *width: 100%/9* to each image. Bootstrap does not do this automatically, because it has disadvantages for other formats.

```
1 < img src="..." class="img-fluid" alt="Responsive
image">
```

It is easy to put images in special forms when using the thumbnails *img-thumbnail* class (Figure 6-6):

```
1    <img src="..." alt="..." class="img-thumbnail">
```

Figure 6-6. *Thumbnail effects on pictures*

Embedded Sources

Embedded sources for video, audio, or external HTML pages are based on <iframe>-, <embed>-, <video>-, and <audio> elements.

The commonly used attributions, such as frameborder="0" for frames, are supplied automatically. The class *embed-responsive* is used with an additional class that specifies the correct display and format:

- *.embed-responsive-16by9*: Format 16:9

- *.embed-responsive-4by3*: Format 4:3

```
1   <!-- 16:9 aspect ratio -->
2   <div class="embed-responsive embed-responsive-16by9">
3     <iframe class="embed-responsive-item"
      src="..."></iframe>
4   </div>
5
6   <!-- 4:3 aspect ratio -->
7   <div class="embed-responsive embed-responsive-4by3">
8     <iframe class="embed-responsive-item"
      src="..."></iframe>
9   </div>
```

Colors and Backgrounds

Colors and backgrounds are global, so they provide variations of elements that have been provided.

Text Color

Text colors are classes that have a slightly semantic meaning (see Listing 6-3 and Figure 6-7). The primary classes are as follows:

- *text-muted*: suppressed, bright, and gray.

- *text-primary*: primary, main action, or primary statement, blue, important.

- *text-success*: success, green, positive, or success.

- *text-info*: information, azure, highlight, attention needed.

- *text-warning*: warning, orange, action is consequential or message is critical.

- *text-danger*: danger, red, errors or irreversible, serious warning.

Listing 6-3. Colors for Text (Text_Colors.html)

```
<p class="text-muted">...</p>
<p class="text-primary">...</p>
<p class="text-success">...</p>
<p class="text-info">...</p>
<p class="text-warning">...</p>
<p class="text-danger">...</p>
```

```
Muted

Primary

Success

Info

Warning

Danger
```

Figure 6-7. *Text colors*

When allocated to an item, <p> is just another example that does not have the desired effect, and the use of another <span> element may be helpful. It is true that the weak semantic meaning is not accessible and screen readers do not reflect this information. Additional details that are hidden with *.sr-only* are the right solution.

The semantic text classes are complemented by some variations of black and white:

```
<p class="text-light bg-dark">Light needs dark background</p>
<p class="text-dark">Dark color (almost black)</p>
<p class="text-body">Black</p>
<p class="text-muted">Gray</p>
<p class="text-white bg-dark">White</p>
<p class="text-black-50">50% of Black is light gray</p>
<p class="text-white-50 bg-dark">50% of white is light gray</p>
```

Background Color

Available background colors are similar classes that have a slightly semantic meaning (see Figure 6-8). The primary criteria are as follows:

- *Primary*: primary, main action or primary statement, blue.

- *Success*: success, green, positive or success.

- *Info*: information, violet, highlight, attention needed.

- *Warning*: warning, orange, action is consequential or message is critical.

- *Danger*: danger, red, errors or irreversible, serious warning.

```
<p class="bg-faded">...</p>
<p class="bg-primary">...</p>
<p class="bg-success">...</p>
<p class="bg-info">...</p>
<p class="bg-warning">...</p>
<p class="bg-danger">...</p>
```

Figure 6-8. *Background colors*

When allocating to an item, <p> here is an example that does not have the desired effect, so the use of another <div> element can be helpful. The weak semantic meaning is not appropriate for accessibility and screen readers do not reflect this information. Again, additional details that are hidden with *.sr-only* are the right solution.

The background has a nonsemantic set, too. This includes the following classes:

- bg-light

- bg-dark

- bg-white

- bg-transparent

Alignment of Elements in Flow

The natural flow (sequence of elements) on a page can be changed by the classes *.float-xx-left* and *.float-xx-right*. The element is always pulled to the right or left edge, even if this means the natural order is changed. Internally, it is based on the style rule float.

The placeholder "xx" must be replaced with a breakpoint hint, such as "sm," "md," or "lg." The element will be arranged if the breakpoint applies.

```
<div class="float-left">...</div>
<div class="float-right">...</div>
```

This should not be done in navigation bars, where there are the specific classes *.navbar-left* or *.navbar-right*.

Aligning Text

With *text-center* an element in the container is centered (with or without breakpoint infixes):

```
1    <div class="text-md-center">...</div>
```

The element <center> is deprecated and should no longer be used with HTML 5.

You can also use *.text-left* and *.text-right*, respectively. To justify the text in a container where multiple lines are shown, consider using *.text-justify*.

Wrapping and Overflow

One task a developer often has trouble with is controlling wrapping and overflow. This happens when the content is too big for the given container. Particularly in sites where the content is dynamic, it is often hard to predict how the elements look like in production. To control this, use the classes *.text-wrap* or *.text-nowrap*. With wrapping you allow the content to respect the width of the container and wrap at word boundaries. The element will grow vertically. With suppressed wrapping the content will exceed the element to the right, but the container remains the same. This behavior is called overflow. To cut the content, use *.text-truncate*. The part outside the container element will become invisible.

If a long word exceeds the container and wrapping is on, the result is a break in the middle of a word. That could render text unreadable. Here the class *.text-break* overrides the behavior and the long word "wins." The container might still not have enough space, and therefore a horizontal scrollbar appears. That's generally not attractive, but it keeps text readable.

Transformation and Font Weight

You can transform text in components with text capitalization classes:

- lowercased text.

- UPPERCASED TEXT.

- Capitalized Text.

The option capitalized transforms the first letter into uppercase form. The other letters remain unchanged, regardless of their casing.

For fonts some weight can be applied:

```
<p class="font-weight-bold">Bold text.</p>
<p class="font-weight-bolder">Bolder weight text (relative to
the parent element).</p>
<p class="font-weight-normal">Normal weight text.</p>
<p class="font-weight-light">Light weight text.</p>
<p class="font-weight-lighter">Lighter weight text (relative to
the parent element).</p>
<p class="font-italic">Italic text.</p>
```

Use this carefully, as not all fonts support all styles. There is always a fallback, so text will remain readable. But if you use font weights to emphasize parts of the text, a missing style would make it hard or impossible to recognize.

A special form of transformation is *.text-monospace*. This is a nonproportional font, where each letter has the same width, making it perfect for code listings.

Break: Clearfix

To interrupt the flow, use *.clearfix* on the parent element.

```
1    <div class="clearfix">...</div>
```

193

To break the flow of the HTML elements, you can easily use *display:block*. In fact this belongs to the eternal clearfix history, and is one of the most complex hacks in the CSS world. So what is behind it? First, the definition in Bootstrap's Sass source code:

```
1   @mixin clearfix() {
2      &::after {
3        content: "";
4        display: table;
5        clear: both;
6      }
7   }
```

This code produces pseudoelements and sets the display mode to *table*. This creates an anonymous table cell in block format. The :before rule prevents the upper edge from collapsing with the previous element. This prevents a "stranger" distance that is disturbing. The :after rule generates the actual movement of the item onto the next line.

Even more powerful are the float-classes (.float-none, .float-left, .float-right) for alignment of elements outside their regular order. All these classes have variations to activate for certain breakpoints.

Show and Hide Content

With the class *.text-hide*, text contents are explicitly hidden. The application succeeds only for block elements, such as <div>. Other styles still apply, so it can be used to replace text portions with a background image, for instance.

```
1   <div class="text-hide"
2      style="background-image: url('/assets/logo.svg');
       width: 50px; height: 50px;">Text replaced with Logo
       </div>
```

Showing or hiding can also be made dependent on the device width. For this purpose, the following classes are used ("<>" are placeholders):

- *.d-none:* hide on all breakpoints

- *.d-sm-none*: hide only with "sm"

- *.d-md-none*: hide only with "md"

- *.d-lg-none*: hide only with "lg"

- *.d-xl-none*: hide only with "xl"

The classes are then available in three variants ("<>" is a placeholder for breakpoint information):

- *.d-<>-block: display: block;*

Printer Support

Comparable to the code for the screen, content can be shown or hidden when printing, too:

- *.d-print-block*

- *.d-print-inline*

- *.d-print-inline-block*

- *.d-print-table*

- *.d-print-none*

The final document class looks (for example) like this: *.visible-xs-block*. The area that is designated will be displayed only if the screen is less than 768 px wide.

Summary

In this chapter we covered a few basic styles for common situations, such as text and background colors, alignment, and justification. Most classes can be used almost everywhere and can complement others.

CHAPTER 7

Components

Components are the building blocks taken from the Bootstrap library, and they provide certain functionalities that go beyond the mere use of CSS. Components are made from CSS with a combination of HTML, JavaScript, and font libraries.

Requirements

Some of the components require support by JavaScript libraries. In the current version of Bootstrap, version 4.5, this is *jQuery* and *popper.js*. You must load the libraries in the required order to get it working.

```
1   <script src="assets/jquery.js"></script>
2   <script src="assets/popper.js"></script>
3   <script src="assets/bootstrap.js"></script>
```

This example assumes that you have copied the files into the production folder *assets*. Adjust the folders to match your build environment. In future versions of Bootstrap there are plans to replace the external dependencies with code delivered by Bootstrap directly.

© Jörg Krause 2020
J. Krause, *Introducing Bootstrap 4*, https://doi.org/10.1007/978-1-4842-6203-0_7

Drop-Down Menus

Drop-downs—context or pop-up menus—are an integral part of many forms. The interaction is complex and partly based on JavaScript. It must not be activated separately; the data-attributes attach here, namely data-toggle="dropdown." Even menus benefit from symbols.

In Bootstrap 4 menus are not created with <ul><li></li></ul> any longer, but with <div> and regular buttons or anchor tags that match *.dropdown-menu* or *.dropdown-item*, and information can be added to them (see Listing 7-1 and Figure 7-1).

Listing 7-1. Menu Folds Downward (Part of Icons_DropDown. html)

```
1   <div class="dropdown">
2     <button class="btn btn-primary dropdown-toggle"
3             type="button"
4             id="dropdownMenu1"
5             data-toggle="dropdown"
6             aria-haspopup="true" aria-expanded="true">
7      Fold down
8      <span class="caret"></span>
9     </button>
10    <div class="dropdown-menu" aria-
      labelledby="dropdownMenu1">
11     <a class="dropdown-item" href="#">Edit</a>
12     <a class="dropdown-item" href="#">Delete</a>
13     <a class="dropdown-item" href="#">Details</a>
14     <a class="dropdown-item" href="#">Lock</a>
15    </div>
16  </div>
```

Figure 7-1. *Menu folds downward*

With the class *.dropup* the menu can fold to the top instead (see Listing 7-2 and Figure 7-2).

Listing 7-2. Menu Tilted Upward (Part of Icons_DropDown.html)

```
1   <div class="dropup">
2     <button class="btn btn-secondary dropdown-toggle"
3                   type="button"
4           id="dropdownMenu3" data-toggle="dropdown"
5           aria-haspopup="true" aria-expanded="false">
6       Fold Up
7     </button>
8     <div class="dropdown-menu" aria-
      labelledby="dropdownMenu2">
9       <a class="dropdown-item" href="#">Edit</a>
10      <a class="dropdown-item" href="#">Delete</a>
11      <a class="dropdown-item" href="#">Detail</a>
12      <a class="dropdown-item" href="#">Block</a>
13    </div>
14  </div>
```

Edit

Delete

Detail

Block

Fold Up 👆

Figure 7-2. *Menu tilted upward*

The ability to "fold up" is limited to available space. If the button is at the top of the page and the menu would exceed the browser's boundaries, it will fold down. This will not change the icon, which is still showing upwards.

Alignment of the Menu

A normal menu is left-aligned. With *.dropdown-menu-right* it can be changed to be aligned right to the button (see Listing 7-3 and Figure 7-3; the inner part of the drop-down's div container is the same as in Listing 7-2). If an alignment is completed in a parent element that needs to be changed, use *.dropdown-menu-left*.

Listing 7-3. Alignment in the Container (Excerpt from Icons_ DropDown_Right.html)

```
1   <div class="dropdown-menu dropdown-menu-right"
2       aria-labelledby="dLabel">
3       ...
4   </div>
```

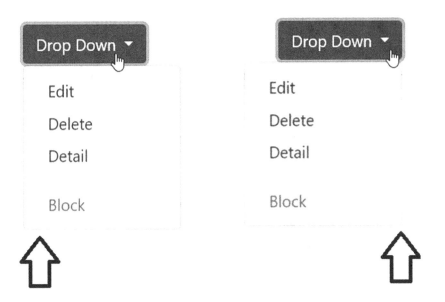

Figure 7-3. *Alignment related to the button element (left and right)*

Decorative Elements

Decorative elements complement the menus. They should be used primarily to improve the readability of long menus and not simply as decoration.

Subheads in Menus

Inactive subheadings can be added for decoration. A normal heading element of suitable size can be used; <h6> usually works very well (see Listing 7-4 and Figure 7-4).

Listing 7-4. Subtitle (Icons_Dropdown_Header.html)

```
1    <div class="dropdown">
2      <button class="btn btn-primary dropdown-toggle"
       type="button"
3              id="dropdownMenu2" data-toggle="dropdown"
4              aria-haspopup="true" aria-expanded="true">
5        Fold Down
6      </button>
7      <div class="dropdown-menu dropdown-menu-left" aria-
       labelledby="dropdownMenu1">
8        <a class="dropdown-item" href="#">Edit</a>
9        <a class="dropdown-item" href="#">Delete</a>
10       <a class="dropdown-item" href="#">Detail</a>
11       <h6 class="dropdown-header">Important</h6>
12       <a class="dropdown-item" href="#">Block</a>
13     </div>
14   </div>
```

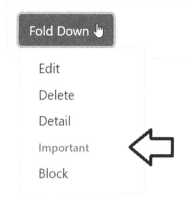

Figure 7-4. *Adding a subtitle*

Divider Line

Separator lines can be used to optically separate a series of links (see Listing 7-5 and Figure 7-5). This makes long menus easier to read. You can achieve this effect with the class *dropdown-divider*. As an alternative, you can also use <hr />.

Listing 7-5. Divider Line (Icons_DropDown_Sep.html)

```
1   <div class="dropdown">
2     <button
3       class="btn btn-primary dropdown-toggle"
4       type="button"
5       id="dropdownMenu2"
6       data-toggle="dropdown"
7       aria-haspopup="true"
8       aria-expanded="true"
9     >
10      Fold Down
11    </button>
12    <div class="dropdown-menu dropdown-menu-left" aria-
      labelledby="dropdownMenu1">
13      <a class="dropdown-item" href="#">Edit</a>
14      <a class="dropdown-item" href="#">Delete</a>
15      <a class="dropdown-item" href="#">Detail</a>
16      <div role="separator" class="dropdown-divider"></div>
17      <a class="dropdown-item" href="#">Block</a>
18    </div>
19  </div>
20  </div>
```

Figure 7-5. *Divider line*

Deactivated Links

You can disable <li> a menu item with *.disabled.* Listing 7-6 and Figure 7-6 shows the method and the results.

Listing 7-6. Deactivated Entry (Icons_DropDown_Dis.html, partially)

```
1    <div class="dropdown">
2      <button
3        class="btn btn-secondary dropdown-toggle"
4        type="button"
5        id="dropdownMenu1"
6        data-toggle="dropdown"
7        aria-haspopup="true"
8        aria-expanded="true"
9      >
10     Drop Down
11     </button>
```

```
12    <div class="dropdown-menu" aria-
      labelledby="dropdownMenu1">
13      <a class="dropdown-item" href="#">Edit</a>
14      <a class="dropdown-item" href="#">Delete</a>
15      <a class="dropdown-item" href="#">Detail</a>
16      <div role="separator" class="dropdown-divider"></div>
17      <a class="dropdown-item disabled" href="#"
        tabindex="-1" aria-disabled="true">Block</a>
18    </div>
19  </div>
```

Figure 7-6. *Deactivated entry*

The mouse pointer is set to a neutral pointer, while active entries show a hand.

Toolbars

Toolbars are technically groups of buttons. The buttons are horizontally next to each other. Embedded checkboxes, drop-downs, and radio buttons require JavaScript to work correctly. For drop-downs the additional library *popper.js* is a requirement.

205

Tooltips and superimposed dialogs (pop-overs) need special settings—container: 'body' in the options section of JavaScript—to specify where the item should dock at the DOM to trigger the rendering process. *body* is most the suitable. However, each container element can be addressed.

```
1   $("#testsettracesBtn1").popover({
2       container: 'body'
3   });
```

The semantic meaning is supported with the role-attribute, either role="group" or role="toolbar." As discussed in previous chapters, this is an useful support to screen readers and is achieved with `aria-label` or `aria-labelledby`.

```
1   <div class="btn-group" role="group" aria-label="...">
2       <button type="button" class="btn btn-
        default">Left</button>
3       <button type="button" class="btn btn-
        default">Mid</button>
4       <button type="button" class="btn btn-
        default">Right</button>
5   </div>
```

Complex toolbars may be built with a combination of <div class="btn-group"> within <div class="btn-toolbar">.

```
1   <div class="btn-toolbar" role="toolbar" aria-label="">
2       <div class="btn-group" role="group" aria-
        label="">...</div>
3       <div class="btn-group" role="group" aria-
        label="">...</div>
4       <div class="btn-group" role="group" aria-
        label="">...</div>
5   </div>
```

With the *.btn-group*-group-classes a complete set of buttons can be made with resize.

The usual suffixes "sm," "md," "lg," and so on are available; the default value is "md."

```
1   <div class="btn-group btn-group-lg"
2   role="group"
3   aria-label="...">...
4   </div>
5   <div class="btn-group"
6   role="group"
7   aria-label="..."> 7    ...
8   </div>
9   <div class="btn-group btn-group-sm"
10  role="group"
11  aria-label="...">
12  ...
13  </div>
14  <div class="btn-group btn-group-lg"
15  role="group"
16  aria-label="...">
17      ...
18  </div>
```

To create buttons with combined pop-up menus, you can nest the *.btn-group-* classes, as in Listing 7-7 and Figure 7-7:

Listing 7-7. Toolbar with Buttons (Toolbar.html)

```
1   <div class="btn-toolbar" role="toolbar" aria-
    label="Toolbar">
2     <div class="btn-group" role="group">
3       <button type="button"
4               class="btn btn-secondary dropdown-toggle"
```

```
 5                   data-toggle="dropdown"
 6                   aria-haspopup="true"
 7                   aria-expanded="false">
 8         Sort
 9           <span class="caret"></span>
10         </button>
11         <div class="dropdown-menu">
12           <a class="dropdown-item" href="#">Descending</a>
13           <a class="dropdown-item" href="#">Ascending</a>
14         </div>
15       </div>
16     <div class="btn-group" role="group">
17       <button class="btn btn-danger">Delete</button>
18     </div>
19     <div class="btn-group" role="group">
20       <button class="btn btn-primary">Detail</button>
21     </div>
```

Figure 7-7. *Toolbar with buttons*

Vertical Alignment

The assumption so far has been that toolbars always ran horizontally.
If you place them on the edge, it is better to place them vertically.
Listing 7-8 shows how to do it. The library *Font Awesome* is used for the
symbols here. The corresponding CSS must also be involved.

Listing 7-8. Vertical Toolbar with Buttons (Toolbar_Vertical.html)

```
1   <div class="btn-toolbar" role="toolbar"
2        aria-label="Toolbar">
3     <div class="btn-group-vertical" role="group">
4       <button class="btn btn-info">
5         <span class="fa fa-plus"></span>
6       </button>
7       <button class="btn btn-info">
8         <span class="fa fa-minus"></span>
9       </button>
10      <button class="btn btn-danger">Delete</button>
11      <button class="btn btn-primary">Detail</button>
12    </div>
13  </div>
```

Shared buttons (aka SplitButton) or pop-up menus cannot be used; the menus are misplaced. Figure 7-8 shows a vertical toolbar with buttons.

Figure 7-8. *Vertical toolbar with buttons*

General Options

You can apply some effects overall to the toolbars. To navigate within a page the <a>-Tag is used, but it is formatted as a button. It is important here to maintain a semantic reference and use the attribute role="button."

```
1    <div class="btn-group"
2        role="group" aria-label="...">
3      <a class="btn btn-primary" role="button"
4        href="#">Return</a>
5      <a class="btn btn-primary" role="button" href="#">2</a>
6      <a class="btn btn-primary" role="button"
       href="#">End</a>
7    </div>
```

Menu Button

Each button can trigger pop-up menus. The button can appear in one or two parts. This requires you to add the *popper.js* library.

Simple Button with Menu

The arrangement must be in a *.btn-group*-class. The function requires JavaScript. If you do not use the entire library, the *DropDown-Plugin* is required (see Listing 7-9 and Figure 7-9).

Listing 7-9. Toolbar with Drop-Down Menu (Toolbar_DropDown. html)

```
1    <div class="btn-toolbar" role="toolbar" aria-
     label="Toolbar">
2      <div class="btn-group" role="group">
3        <button type="button" class="btn btn-
         secondary">File</button>
4      </div>
```

```
5    <div class="btn-group" role="group">
6      <button type="button"
7              class="btn btn-secondary dropdown-toggle"
8              data-toggle="dropdown"
9              aria-haspopup="true" aria-expanded="false">
10       Action <span class="caret"></span>
11     </button>
12     <div class="dropdown-menu">
13       <a class="dropdown-item" href="#">Show</a>
14       <a class="dropdown-item" href="#">Moving</a>
15       <a class="dropdown-item" href="#">Copy</a>
16       <div role="separator" class="dropdown-
         divider"></div>
17       <a class="dropdown-item" href="#">Delete</a>
18     </div>
19   </div>
20  </div>
```

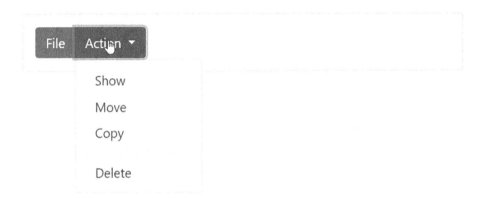

Figure 7-9. *Toolbar with drop-down menu*

The trigger for JavaScript is the attribute `data-toggle="dropdown"` (line 4). The black triangle image on the menu option is produced with the class *.caret* (line 6).

Split-Button Menu

A split button (SplitButton) is created simply with a further <button>-element. Usually, such a button triggers a default option from the list of options offered from a menu (see Listing 7-10 and Figure 7-10).

Listing 7-10. Toolbar with Split Button (Toolbar_Split.html)

```
1   <div class="btn-toolbar" role="toolbar" aria-
    label="Toolbar">
2     <div class="btn-group">
3       <button type="button"
4   class="btn btn-danger">Standard</button>
5       <button type="button" class="btn btn-danger dropdown-
        toggle"
6               data-toggle="dropdown"
7               aria-haspopup="true" aria-expanded="false">
8         <span class="caret"></span>
9         <span class="sr-only">Open Menu</span>
10      </button>
11      <div class="dropdown-menu">
12        <a class="dropdown-item" href="#">Standard</a>
13        <a class="dropdown-item" href="#">More</a>
14        <a class="dropdown-item" href="#">Even more</a>
15        <div role="separator" class="dropdown-divider"></div>
16        <a class="dropdown-item" href="#">Others</a>
17      </div>
18    </div>
19  </div>
```

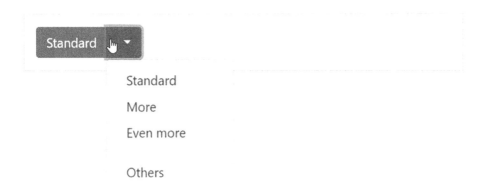

Figure 7-10. *Toolbar with split button*

Sizes of Menu Buttons

Basically, you can use any size of menu buttons (see Listing 7-11 and Figure 7-11). The menu adapts to the styles *btn-lg* and *btn-sm*. However, *btn-md* is the default and does not need to be specified.

Listing 7-11. Menu Sizes (Toolbar_Size.html)

```
1   <div class="btn-group">
2       <button class="btn btn-secondary btn-lg dropdown-
        toggle"
3               type="button" data-toggle="dropdown"
4               aria-haspopup="true" aria-expanded="false">
5         Huge <span class="caret"></span>
6       </button>
7       <div class="dropdown-menu">
8         ...
9       </div>
10  </div>
11
```

```
12   <div class="btn-group">
13     <button class="btn btn-secondary dropdown-toggle"
14             type="button" data-toggle="dropdown"
15             aria-haspopup="true" aria-expanded="false">
16       Normal <span class="caret"></span>
17     </button>
18     <div class="dropdown-menu">
19       ...
20     </div>
21   </div>
22
23   <div class="btn-group">
24     <button class="btn btn-secondary btn-sm dropdown-toggle"
25             type="button" data-toggle="dropdown"
26             aria-haspopup="true" aria-expanded="false">
27       Small <span class="caret"></span>
28     </button>
29     <div class="dropdown-menu">
30       ...
31     </div>
32   </div>
```

Figure 7-11. *Menu sizes*

Note that the details have been changed as compared to those from Bootstrap 3. The smallest form is "sm."

214

Special Menu Options

With the help of the class *.dropup*, the menu can be made visible upwards.

```
1    <div class="btn-group dropup">
2      <button type="button" class="btn btn-secondary">
3        Folding
4      </button>
5      <button type="button"
6              class="btn btn-default dropdown-toggle"
7              data-toggle="dropdown"
8              aria-haspopup="true" aria-expanded="false">
9          <span class="caret"></span>
10         <span class="sr-only">open menu</span>
11       </button>
12     <div class="dropdown-menu">
13       <!-- Here are menu items -->
14   </div>
```

Navigation

The navigation elements are all initiated by a common base class *.nav*. When navigating by tabulators, JavaScript is required. To support the accessibility attribute, role="navigation" should be used in the logic overlying containers. This gives the navigation the necessary semantic meaning. The important thing is not to do so on the <ul>- element, but on the surrounding <nav> or <div> element.

Basically, distinction should be made in navigation between content navigation and navigation action. Content can be accessed via links, buttons, or tabs. However, navigation action takes place over buttons, menus, toolbars, menu strips, and so on. Forms are among the content. Only the submit button, for example, is an action.

Tabs

Tabs are an ideal way to logically separate multiple forms or compartmentalize a large form into manageable areas (see Listing 7-12 and Figure 7-12).

Listing 7-12. Tabs (Nav_Tab.html)

```
 1   <ul class="nav nav-tabs">
 2       <li class="nav-item" role="presentation">
 3           <a data-toggle="tab" class="nav-link active" href="#">
 4           Start
 5           </a>
 6       </li>
 7       <li class="nav-item" role="presentation">
 8           <a data-toggle="tab" class="nav-link" href="#">
 9           Profile
10           </a>
11       </li>
12       <li class="nav-item" role="presentation">
13           <a data-toggle="tab" class="nav-link" href="#">
14           News
15           </a>
16       </li>
17   </ul>
```

Note here the positioning of classes *.nav-item* and *.nav-link*.

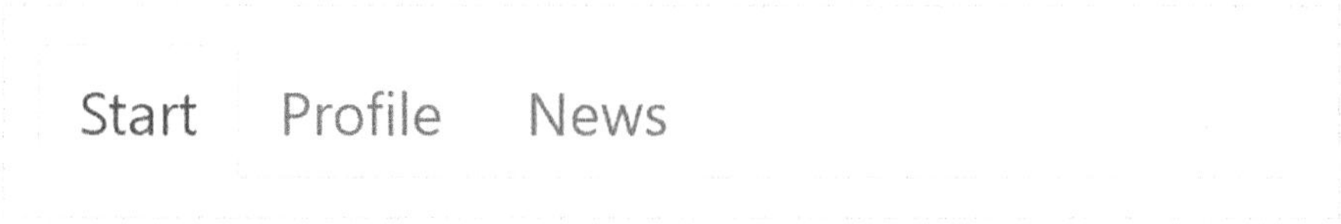

Start   Profile   News

Figure 7-12. *Tabs*

The activating element is the attribute data-toggle="tab." Tabs that are to be activated with their own code do not carry this attribute.

Navigation Buttons (Pills)

Pills are buttons that function as navigation items, just like the tabs. To activate them the class *.nav-pills* is required, and a structure identical to the tabulators. This results in a more button-like design, as shown in Listing 7-13.

Listing 7-13. Navigation Buttons (Nav_Pills.html)

```
1    <ul class="nav nav-pills">
2      <li role="presentation" class="nav-item">
3        <a href="#" class="nav-link active" data-
           toggle="pill">
4          Start
5        </a>
6      </li>
7      <li role="presentation" class="nav-item">
8        <a class="nav-link" data-toggle="pill" href="#">
9        Profile
10       </a>
11     </li>
12     <li role="presentation" class="nav-item">
13       <a class="nav-link" data-toggle="pill" href="#">
14       News
15       </a>
16     </li>
17   </ul>
```

Note in Figure 7-13 the positioning of classes *.nav-item* and *.nav-link*.

Figure 7-13. *Navigation buttons (pills)*

The pills elements mentioned can also be arranged vertically. For this purpose, *.nav-stacked* is added.

```
1   <ul class="nav nav-pills nav-stacked">
2     ...
3 </ul>
```

JavaScript is required for full functionality. Bootstrap brings the code. It is activated via the attribute `data-toggle="pill."` Tabs that are to be activated with their own code do not carry this attribute.

Universal Settings

Universal settings affect all navigation elements. This concerns the following:

- Orientation
- Deactivation
- Folding menus

Orientation

All items that can be placed horizontally suffer when viewed if the content differs drastically. It feels more natural when the elements use the space to the utmost. To facilitate the decision, a broad representation engages up to a 768 px screen width. The elements are distributed uniformly over the entire screen, similar to justification. The effect can be achieved with *.nav-justified*. On wider screens, the elements are placed left-aligned.

```
1   <ul class="nav nav-tabs nav-justified">
2     ...
3   </ul>
4   <ul class="nav nav-pills nav-justified">
5     ...
6   </ul>
```

Deactivation

It may happen that the content in question or part of the form does not need to be reached. In this case the item is disabled (see Listing 7-14 and Figure 7-14). It is then grayed out and does not respond to the mouse or touch actions.

Listing 7-14. Disabled Navigation Buttons (Nav_Pills_Disabled. html)

```
1   <ul class="nav nav-pills">
2     ...
3   <li role="presentation" class="nav-item">
4   <a class="nav-link disabled" href="#">Deactivated Link</a>
5   </li>
6     ...
7   </ul>
```

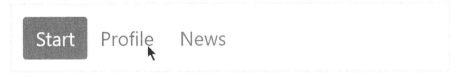

Figure 7-14. *Disabled navigation buttons*

The mouse pointer is neutral on the disabled element, while it is a hand on active entries.

Expansion Through Pop-Up Menus

Tabs can be expanded by folding menus (see Listing 7-15 and Figure 7-15). However, you should certainly think twice about this, because it makes using the feature complicated and is not a typical menu position. The user might not realize the intended function.

Listing 7-15. Navigation Buttons with (Nav_TabMenu.html)

```
1   <ul class="nav nav-tabs">
2     <li role="presentation" class="nav-item">
3       <a class="nav-link active" href="#"
4           data-toggle="tab">Files
5       </a>
6     </li>
7     <li role="presentation" class="nav-item dropdown">
8       <a class="nav-link dropdown-toggle"
9           data-toggle="dropdown"
10          href="#" role="button"
11          aria-haspopup="true"
12          aria-expanded="false">
13        Quick Menu <span class="caret"></span>
14      </a>
15      <div class="dropdown-menu">
16          <a class="dropdown-item" href="#">Loading</a>
17          <a class="dropdown-item" href="#">Unloading</a>
18      </div>
19    </li>
```

```
20    <li role="presentation" class="nav-item">
21       <a class="nav-link" href="#" data-
         toggle="tab">Backup</a>
22    </li>
23    </ul>
```

Files	Quick Menu ▼	Backup
	Loading	
	Unloading	

Figure 7-15. *Navigation buttons with menu*

Moreover, the drop-down menu can be used with either data-toggle="dropdown" foldable or data-toggle="tab." So it has either the behavior of a tab or a menu, but not both. A pull-down menu without a menu function is meaningless, so the only option is to use a part of the menu tabs without the tab function (a rare need).

Pills can do this as well, and behave in an identical way:

```
1    <ul class="nav nav-pills">
2    ...
3    <li role="presentation" class="nav-item dropdown">
4    <a class="nav-link dropdown-toggle"
5    data-toggle="dropdown" href="#"
6    role="button"
7    aria-haspopup="true" aria-expanded="false">
8    Dropdown <span class="caret"></span>
9    </a>
```

```
10   <div class="dropdown-menu">
11   ...
12   </div>
13   </li>
14   ...
15   </ul>
```

Navigation Bar

The navigation bar (navbar) is a highly responsive element. You usually begin with a page that has complex content, with a menu bar at the top (see Listing 7-16). If the width is too small, the items will be outside the visible area (they vanish at the right side) and they are hence inaccessible by the user. This is where Bootstrap completely rebuilds the navigation bar. For this purpose, the elements are now arranged vertically and if the user decreases the view in the width further, the menu bar does not cover the entire page width.

What cannot be immediately solved is the width of the content. Without intervention, the headings on the navigation elements do not fit and will wrap around another line. This enlarges the menu downwards and it will eventually run out of the view. Because of the complexity and the strong engagement in the design of the page, this requires manual rework, and Bootstrap only provides the framework. Possible additional measures are the following:

- Reduce the number of elements—must all elements really be accessible from the first page?

- Depending on the width of the screen elements, they may be hidden dynamically—perhaps some functions are not useful for a small screen?

- Adjust the menus targeted to all screens, possibly through their own media spaces.

The collapse of the broad menu to narrow requires JavaScript. You don't need to add all components, as this feature is available through the collapse plug-in. The switch between narrow and wide defaults to 768 px.

The matching attributes for barrier-free access should be used in particular role="navigation."

Listing 7-16. Navigation Buttons with Menu (Nav_Navbar.html))

```
1    <nav class="navbar navbar-dark navbar-expand-lg
     bg-primary">
2      <div class="container-fluid">
3        <div class="navbar-header">
4          <button type="button" class="navbar-toggler d-lg-none"
5                    data-toggle="collapse"
6                    data-target="#n1"
7                    aria-expanded="false">
8              <span class="sr-only">Logo</span>
9
10         </button>
11         <a class="navbar-brand" href="#">Logo</a>
12       </div>
13       <div class="collapse navbar-collapse" id="n1">
14         <ul class="nav navbar-nav">
15           <li class="nav-item active">
16             <a class="nav-link" href="#">
17         File
18         <span class="sr-only">File</span>
19               </a>
20           </li>
21           <li class="nav-item dropdown">
22             <a href="#" class="nav-link dropdown-toggle"
23                    data-toggle="dropdown"
```

```
24              role="button"
25              aria-haspopup="true" aria-expanded="false">
26          Functions <span class="caret"></span>
27            </a>
28          <div class="dropdown-menu">
29            <a class="dropdown-item" href="#">Copy</a>
30            <a class="dropdown-item" href="#">Move</a>
31            <a class="dropdown-item" href="#">Show</a>
32            <div role="separator" class="dropdown-
                divider"></div>
33            <a class="dropdown-item" href="#">Delete</a>
34            <div role="separator" class="dropdown-
                divider"></div>
35             <a class="dropdown-item" href="#">Rename</a>
36          </div>
37        </li>
38      </ul>
39
40      <form class="form-inline navbar-form navbar-left"
41            role="search">
42        <div class="form-group">
43          <input type="text" class="form-control"
44                  placeholder="Keyword">
45        </div>
46        <button type="submit" class="btn btn-secondary">
47          Search
48        </button>
49      </form>
50    </div>
51  </div>
52 </nav>
```

The navigation bar is introduced with a logo or symbol. At this point, text or images may appear (see Figures 7-16 and 7-17).

Figure 7-16. *Navigation bar (full width, Listing 7-16)*

The typical icon for a collapsed menu on small screens is called a "hamburger icon." Instead of a font in the example, an UTF-8 character is used to present this. This might not be available in other fonts.

Figure 7-17. *Navigation bar with a small screen (Listing 7-16)*

The color options for the navigation bar include a common dark and light mode using these classes:

- *.navbar-dark*

- *.navbar-light*

These classes define the foreground color. For this to work a matching background color, for example *.bg-primary*, must be selected.

Form Elements

Navigation bars sometimes offer actions that enable them to not have their own form. For example, search functions as well checkboxes are commonly found on navigation bars. With *form-inline* and margin utilities, the matching distances are configured. The form element is aligned within the navigation element.

```
1   <form class="form-inline " role="search">
2     <div class="form-group">
3       <input type="text"
4           class="form-control"
5           placeholder="Keyword" />
6     </div>
7     <button type="submit" class="btn btn-secondary">
8       Search
9     </button>
10  </form>
```

On a small screen, form elements can rarely be optimally placed. Take separate forms into consideration here, and try to simplify the arrangement further.

Continue to work for barrier-free access even if there is no space in the navigation bar. In such cases using *.sr-only* in combination with `aria-label` and `aria-labelledby` or the `title` attribute is best.

Buttons, Hyperlinks, and Text

Regular buttons are useful to trigger exclusive actions because of their diverse configurability. With *.navbar-link* hyperlinks can be used to fulfill special tasks, such as responding to registration and available page functions, as shown in Listing 7-17 and Figure 7-18.

Listing 7-17. Application Link (Nav_NavbarLink.html)

```
1   <p class="navbar-text ">
2       Logged on as <a href="#" class="navbar-link">
3       Joerg Krause</a>
4   </p>
```

Logged on as Joerg Krause

Figure 7-18. *Application link*

The item appears primarily as text. Content without action, plain text, uses the class *.navbar-text*. The element <p> supports the takeover of the right colors.

```
1   <p class="navbar-text">Registered as Joerg Krause</p>
```

The alignment of the elements is accomplished with *.navbar-left* or *.navbar-right*, respectively. Because the elements usually consist of <li>, the uniform alignment is done on the surrounding <ul>.

Position of the Bar

A discussion occasionally arises over the question of whether the bar constantly remains visible. On the one hand, valuable space is permanently occupied; on the other hand, the user should not be forced to scroll a long way. Some designers solve this dilemma by using two navigation bars. The user first sees a large and elaborately designed one at the top of the page, and then scrolls down to find it replaced by a very narrow, fine, simple bar. Thus, the space requirement is minimal and the navigation is still guaranteed. In each case the bar must be fixed at the top using .*fixed-top*:

```
1    <nav class="navbar navbar-light fixed-top">
2        <div class="container">
3            ...
4    </div>
5    </nav>
```

The bar takes up space on the top of the page, though the definition is usually far deeper. This content is not superimposed intentionally; you may need a total of page height to get the upper distance: body { padding-top: 70px; }

Note   The standard navigation bar (if no theme is used) is 50 px high.

```
1    <nav class="navbar navbar-light navbar-fixed-bottom">
2    <div class="container">
3            ...
4    </div>
5    </nav>
```

A static bar is also at the top of this page, but scrolls upwards. This effect is achieved with .*sticky-top*. A correction of the spacing of the content is not necessary.

```
1    <nav class="navbar navbar-light sticky-top">
2        <div class="container">
3            ...
4    </div>
5    </nav>
```

A reversal of the standard colors is achieved with *.navbar-dark*. You can combine this effect with all other options.

```
1    <nav class="navbar navbar-dark">
2      ...
3    </nav>
```

Breadcrumb Navigation

Complex navigations are often confusing for visitors to the site. The question is always: "Where am I?" The purpose of the navigation path is to enable a path through the navigation hierarchy. This component is referred to as a "breadcrumb" (referencing those used to create a crumb trail). The word "path navigation" is clearer and more appropriate (see Listing 7-18 and Figure 7-19).

Listing 7-18. Breadcrumb Navigation (Nav_Breadcrumb.html)

```
1    <ol class="breadcrumb">
2      <li class="breadcrumb-item"><a href="#">Home</a></li>
3      <li class="breadcrumb-item"><a href="#">Library</a></li>
4      <li class="breadcrumb-item active">Data</li>
5    </ol>
```

Home / Library / Data

Figure 7-19. *Breadcrumb navigation*

Ideally, the path shows not only where the user actually is, but allows navigation as well. Therefore, it is preferable that hyperlinks are used. The active element (class *.active*) is deactivated because the user is already at this location.

Page Scrolling

Even page-by-page scrolling belongs to the navigation elements. Usually it occurs in the context of data tables, but even multipage content pages can be browsed.

A typical setup for a few pages or a reasonably constant number of pages looks like this:

« 1 2 3 4 5 »

Listing 7-19 produces the page scrolling shown in Figure 7-20.

Listing 7-19. Page Scrolling (Nav_Pagination.html)

```
1   <nav>
2   <ul class="pagination">
3   <li class="page-item">
4   <a href="#" aria-label="Previous" class="page-link">
5   <span aria-hidden="true">&laquo;</span>
6   </a>
7   </li>
8   <li class="page-item">
9           <a class="page-link" href="#">1</a></li>
10  <li class="page-item">
11          <a class="page-link" href="#">2</a></li>
12  <li class="page-item">
13          <a class="page-link" href="#">3</a></li>
14  <li class="page-item">
15          <a class="page-link" href="#">4</a></li>
16  <li class="page-item">
17          <a class="page-link" href="#">5</a></li>
```

```
18   <li class="page-item">
19   <a href="#" aria-label="Next" class="page-link">
20   <span aria-hidden="true">&raquo;</span>
21   </a>
22   </li>
23   </ul>
24   </nav>
```

```
« 1 2 3 4 5 »
```

Figure 7-20. *Page scrolling*

If the number of pages is indefinite, sometimes a simple back-and-forth pattern is recommended.

```
1   <nav>
2     <ul class="pager">
3       <li><a href="#">Back</a></li>
4       <li><a href="#">Next</a></li>
5     </ul>
6   </nav>
```

This is even more striking when the solution uses symbols or is complemented with entities, such as in the following example:

```
1   <nav>
2     <ul class="pagination">
3       <li class="page-item prev">
4         <a href="#">
5           <span aria-hidden="true">&larr;</span> Older
6         </a>
7       </li>
```

231

```
 8        <li class="page-item next">
 9          <a href="#">Newer
10            <span aria-hidden="true">&rarr;</span>
11          </a>
12        </li>
13      </ul>
14    </nav>
```

If individual pages are inactive, for example, to display what is currently selected, either *.disabled* or *.active* is being used.

The following code shows how to accomplish this (the output "current" is only for screen readers).

```
 1    <nav>
 2      <ul class="pagination">
 3        <li class="page-item disabled">
 4          <a href="#" aria-label="Previous">
 5            <span aria-hidden="true">&laquo;</span>
 6          </a>
 7        </li>
 8        <li class="active">
 9          <a href="#">1
10            <span class="sr-only">(Current)</span>
11          </a>
12        </li>
13        ...
14      </ul>
15    </nav>
```

A nonselectable option can also be achieved for the arrows, as in Listing 7-20 and shown in Figure 7-21.

Listing 7-20. Simple Leaves (Nav_PaginationON.html)

```
1    <nav>
2      <ul class="pagination">
3        <li class="page-item disabled">
4          <span>
5            <span aria-hidden="true">&laquo;</span>
6          </span>
7        </li>
8        <li class="active">
9          <span>
10           <span class="sr-only">(Current)</span>
11         </span>
12       </li>
13   ...
14     </ul>
15   </nav>
16   <nav>
17     <ul class="pagination">
18       <li class="prev disabled"><a href="#">
19         <span aria-hidden="true">&larr;</span> Older</a>
20       </li>
21       <li class="next">
22         <a href="#">Newer
23           <span aria-hidden="true">&rarr;</span>
24         </a>
25       </li>
26     </ul>
27   </nav>
```

← Older   Newer →

Figure 7-21. *Navigation arrow buttons with partial deactivation*

Size

The default size can be enlarged (*.pagination-lg*) or shrunk (*.pagination-sm*) in one step.

```
1    <nav><ul class="pagination pagination-lg">...</ul></nav>
2    <nav><ul class="pagination">...</ul></nav>
3    <nav><ul class="pagination pagination-sm">...</ul></nav>
```

Add <li> tags for the page numbers and navigation, as shown in the previous examples. This usually depends on code that creates the numbering dynamically, according to the data the user is currently browsing.

Identification Labels (Badges)

Identification labels (badge-pills) are less inflationary when used than regular labels, and they are therefore more exclusive and striking. Their corners are more rounded and they complement the overall picture. When placed on buttons the backgrounds are transparent, so the rounded corners are not visible (see Listing 7-21 and Figure 7-22).

Listing 7-21. Tag-Pills (LabelPillsAnchor.html)

```
1    <a href="#">Inbox
2       <span class="badge badge-pill bg-danger text-white">
3          42
4       </span>
5    </a>
```

```
6    <button class="btn btn-secondary" type="button">
7        <span class="badge badge-pill text-warning">4</span>
         Messages
8    </button>
```

Figure 7-22. *Tag-pills in action*

The application is found mostly in the context of frequently changing data. The user's view is selectively captured. Because possible actions are often hidden behind the presentation of data, it makes sense to embed the badges in the navigation elements. Listing 7-22 shows the number of new messages, and the user can then access the new page by clicking on the item (see Figure 7-23).

Listing 7-22. Bagdes in Navigation (LabelPills.html)

```
1    <ul class="nav nav-pills" role="tablist">
2      <li role="presentation" class="active">
3        <a href="#" data-toggle="pill"
4            class="btn btn-sm btn-primary">
5        Start
6        <span class="badge badge -pill">42</span>
7        </a>
8      </li>
9      <li role="presentation">
10       <a href="#" data-toggle="pill"
11           class="btn btn-sm btn-danger">Profile</a>
12     </li>
```

```
13    <li role="presentation">
14      <a href="#" data-toggle="pill"
15         class="btn btn-sm btn-info">
16      <span class=" badge badge -pill">3</span> Messages
17      </a>
18    </li>
19  </ul>
```

Figure 7-23. *Labels in the navigation*

If the badge has no content, it may render invisible. Consider adding a space entity ( ) or in case of numeric value, show 0 instead of nothing.

The classes available in older Bootstrap versions, such as *.label* or *.tag*, have been deleted to avoid confusion with the <label> element.

Big Screen (Jumbotron)

The jumbotron is a big, bold surface with rounded corners, usually only found on the home page. It contains a slogan, sayings, or product that is presented exclusively, as demonstrated in Listing 7-23 and Figure 7-24.

Listing 7-23. Introduction of a Page (Jumbotron.html)

```
1  <div class="jumbotron">
2  <h1>Hello Bootstrap!</h1>
3  <p>...</p>
4  <p>
5  <a class="btn btn-primary btn-lg"
```

```
6       href="#" role="button">
7             Read more...
8   </a>
9   </p>
10  </div>
```

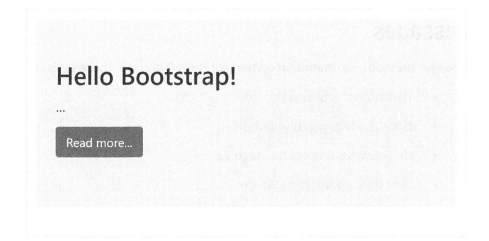

Figure 7-24. *Introduction on a page*

Page Headers

Page headers separate sections, and provide a more comprehensive view than typographic headings alone (see Listing 7-24 and Figure 7-25).

Listing 7-24. Headings with a Dividing Line (PageHeader.html)

```
1   <div class="page-header">
2   <h1>Our Terms
3   <small>Changes</small>
4   </h1>
5   <p>More content</p>
6   </div>
```

237

> **Our Terms** Changes
>
> More content...

Figure 7-25. *Headings with a dividing line*

Messages

Messages provide information in certain contexts. There are these variants:

- *alert-primary*: blue standard

- *alert-secondary*: gray standard

- *alert-success*: success message, green

- *alert-info*: information, azure

- *alert-warning*: warning, orange

- *alert-danger*: error, red

- *alert-light*: neutral light gray on white background

- *alert-dark*: neutral gray background with black text

Messages without a semantic meaning should use the light/dark/primary/secondary variants, because semantic messages should explicitly emphasize a particular state, as shown in Listing 7-25 and Figure 7-26.

Listing 7-25. Output Messages (from Alerts.html, Texts Omitted for Brevity)

```
1   <div class="alert alert-success" role="alert">...</div>
2   <div class="alert alert-info" role="alert">...</div>
3   <div class="alert alert-warning" role="alert">...</div>
4   <div class="alert alert-danger" role="alert">...</div>
```

Figure 7-26. *Output messages*

Because messages often show up without being asked, they should be able to be removed. That is the purpose of the class *.alert-dismissible*, along with a button or an icon for closing. JavaScript is required to do this. The script responds to the attribute `data-dismiss="alert"` (see Listing 7-26 and Figure 7-27).

Listing 7-26. Closable Messages (Alerts_Dismiss.html)

```
1    <div class="alert alert-warning alert-dismissible"
2         role="alert">
3      <button type="button" class="close"
4              data-dismiss="alert" aria-label="Close">
5        <span aria-hidden="true">&times;</span>
6      </button>
7          <strong>Attention!</strong> Please check the data.
8    </div>
```

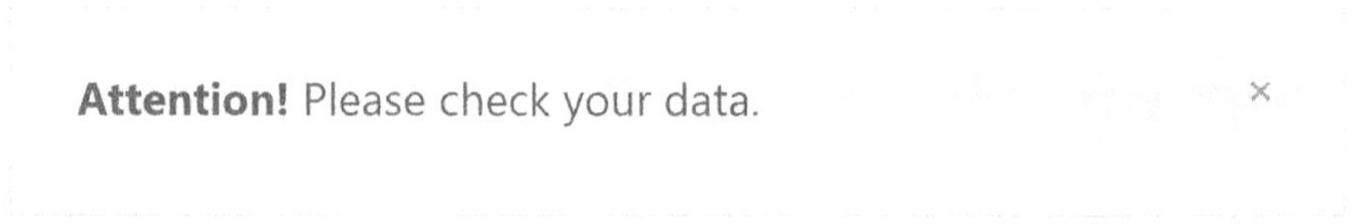

Attention! Please check your data.   ×

Figure 7-27. *Messages that are closable*

Messages that direct the user to further information can be very large. If you use hyperlinks for this purpose, this is accomplished with the class *.alert-link*, shown in Listing 7-27 and Figure 7-28.

Listing 7-27. Messages with Further Link (Alerts_Link.html, Texts Omitted for Brevity)

```
1    <div class="alert alert-success" role="alert">
2      <a href="#" class="alert-link">...</a>
3    </div>
4    <div class="alert alert-info" role="alert">
5      <a href="#" class="alert-link">...</a>
6    </div>
7    <div class="alert alert-warning" role="alert">
8      <a href="#" class="alert-link">...</a>
9    </div>
10   <div class="alert alert-danger" role="alert">
11     <a href="#" class="alert-link">...</a>
12   </div>
```

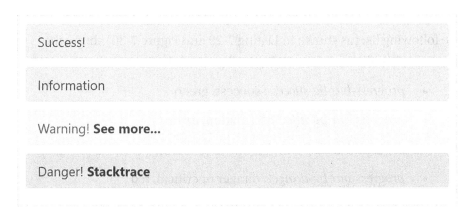

Figure 7-28. *Messages with further link*

Progress Bar

Longer-term actions benefit from the progress bar. The implementation used by Bootstrap is purely a design element that needs to be supplemented for a meaningful indicator with JavaScript. In addition, currently no browsers fully support the required CSS3 and the native HTML element <progress>. A purely CSS driven form is shown in Listing 7-28.

Listing 7-28. Passive Progress Bar (Progress.html)

```
1   <div class="progress">
2     <div class="progress-bar" style="width: 60%"
3         id="val1">60%</div>
4   </div>
```

Note that the actual width of the active zone is generated with a width-style (line 2). This value must be manipulated to move the position of the progress bars (see Figure 7-29).

60%

Figure 7-29. *Passive progress bar*

241

A progress bar can show not only a position, but also a context. The following list (as shown in Listing 7-29 and Figure 7-30) shows the semantically enhanced form using background classes:

- *progress-bar bg-success*: success, green

- *progress-bar bg-info*: information, azure

- *progress-bar bg-warning*: warning, orange

- *progress-bar bg-danger*: danger or critical, red

Listing 7-29. Semantic Progress Bar (Progress_Semantic.html)

```
1   <div class="progress">
2         <div
3            class="progress-bar bg-success"
4            role="progressbar"
5            aria-valuenow="40"
6            aria-valuemin="0"
7            aria-valuemax="100"
8            value="40"
9            style="width: 40%"
10           max="100"
11        >
12           <span class="sr-only">40% Complete (success)
              </span>
13        </div>
14     </div>
15     <div class="progress">
16        <div
17           class="progress-bar bg-info"
18           role="progressbar"
19           aria-valuenow="20"
20           aria-valuemin="0"
```

```
21          aria-valuemax="100"
22          value="20"
23          style="width: 20%"
24          max="100"
25        >
26          <span class="sr-only">20% Complete</span>
27      </div>
28    </div>
29    <div class="progress">
30      <div
31        class="progress-bar bg-warning"
32        role="progressbar"
33        aria-valuenow="60"
34        aria-valuemin="0"
35        aria-valuemax="100"
36        value="60"
37        style="width: 60%"
38        max="100"
39      >
40        <span class="sr-only">60% Complete (warning)
          </span>
41      </div>
42    </div>
43    <div class="progress">
44      <div
45        class="progress-bar bg-danger"
46        role="progressbar"
47        aria-valuenow="80"
48        aria-valuemin="0"
49        aria-valuemax="100"
50        value="80"
51        style="width: 80%"
```

```
52              max="100"
53          >
54              <span class="sr-only">80% Complete (danger)</span>
55          </div>
56          </div>
```

Figure 7-30. *Semantic progress bar*

An obliquely running strip is a nice effect that emphasizes the
animation effect (see Listing 7-30 and Figure 7-31). It works in very slow
running progress bars and unspecific progress bars as well.

Listing 7-30. Semantic with Stripes (Progress_Semantic_Striped.
html)

```
1   <div class="progress">
2       <div
3         class="progress-bar bg-success progress-bar-striped"
4         role="progressbar"
5         aria-valuenow="40"
6         aria-valuemin="0"
7         aria-valuemax="100"
8         value="40"
9         style="width: 40%"
10        max="100"
11      >
12        <span class="sr-only">40% Complete (success)</span>
13      </div>
14      </div>
```

```
15      <div class="progress">
16        <div
17          class="progress-bar bg-info progress-bar-striped"
18          role="progressbar"
19          aria-valuenow="20"
20          aria-valuemin="0"
21          aria-valuemax="100"
22          value="20"
23          style="width: 20%"
24          max="100"
25        >
26          <span class="sr-only">20% Complete</span>
27        </div>
28      </div>
29      <div class="progress">
30        <div
31          class="progress-bar bg-warning progress-bar-striped"
32          role="progressbar"
33          aria-valuenow="60"
34          aria-valuemin="0"
35          aria-valuemax="100"
36          value="60"
37          style="width: 60%"
38          max="100"
39        >
40          <span class="sr-only">60% Complete (warning)</span>
41        </div>
42      </div>
43      <div class="progress">
44        <div
45          class="progress-bar bg-danger progress-bar-striped"
```

```
46              role="progressbar"
47              aria-valuenow="80"
48              aria-valuemin="0"
49              aria-valuemax="100"
50              value="80"
51              style="width: 80%"
52              max="100"
53          >
54              <span class="sr-only">80% Complete (danger)</span>
55          </div>
56        </div>
```

Figure 7-31. *Semantic progress bar with stripes*

More animation can be reached with *.active*, as shown in Figure 7-32.

```
1        <div class="progress">
2            <div
3                class="progress-bar bg-success"
4                id="progress-bar"
5                role="progressbar"
6                aria-valuenow="0"
7                aria-valuemin="0"
8                aria-valuemax="100"
9                value="0"
10               style="width: 50%;"
11               max="100"
12           ></div>
13        </div>
```

```
14        <div>
15          <label class="checkbox-inline"> <input
            type="checkbox" name="inlineRadioOptions"
            id="inlineRadio1" value="1" /> 1 </label>
16          <label class="checkbox-inline"> <input
            type="checkbox" name="inlineRadioOptions"
            id="inlineRadio2" value="2" /> 2 </label>
17          <label class="checkbox-inline"> <input
            type="checkbox" name="inlineRadioOptions"
            id="inlineRadio3" value="3" /> 3 </label>
18          <label class="checkbox-inline"> <input
            type="checkbox" name="inlineRadioOptions"
            id="inlineRadio4" value="4" /> 4 </label>
19          <label class="checkbox-inline"> <input
            type="checkbox" name="inlineRadioOptions"
            id="inlineRadio5" value="5" /> 5 </label>
20          <label class="checkbox-inline"> <input
            type="checkbox" name="inlineRadioOptions"
            id="inlineRadio6" value="6" /> 6 </label>
21        </div>
22      </div>
```

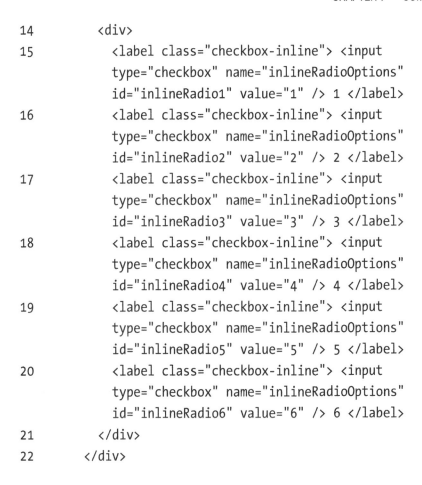

Figure 7-32. *Interactive progress bar*

The behavior is generated by this small script using jQuery (same listing):

```
1   <script>
2     $(function () {
3       var options = $('[name="inlineRadioOptions"]').length;
4       $(':checkbox').on('click', function () {
5         var active = $('[name="inlineRadioOptions"]:check
          ed').length;
6         var value = Math.round((active / options) * 100);
7         $('#progress-bar').css('width', value + '%').
          text(value);
8       });
9     });
10  </script>
```

The script determines the number of options (line 2). Each time you click, the number of active members is determined by a checkbox (line 4). The display and the width are controlled by the calculated percentage. The text in line 9 hides the number 0, so that the display without bars is empty.

Media

Media are videos, audio files, or similar sensitive information.

```
1   <div class="media">
2     <a href="#">
3       <img class="align-self-start" src="..." alt="...">
4     </a>
5     <div class="media-body">
6       <h4 class="media-heading">Media heading</h4>
7         ...
8     </div>
9   </div>
```

The classes *.align-self-start* and *.align-self-end* align the element on the page (top or bottom).

Orientation

Both images and media elements generally line up.

```
1   <div class="media">
2     <a href="#">
3       <img class="align-self-start" src="..." alt="...">
4     </a>
5     <div class="media-body">
6       <h4 class="media-heading">Middle aligned media</h4>
7       ...
8     </div>
9   </div>
```

Media Lists

To organize media in lists, some additional HTML is required.

```
1    <ul class=" list-unstyled">
2      <li class="media">
3        <a href="#">
4          <img class="align-self-start" src="..." alt="...">
5        </a>
6        <div class="media-body">
7          <h4 class="media-heading">Media heading</h4>
10         ...
8        </div>
9      </li>
10   </ul>
```

Common Lists

Lists are grouped collections of elements (see Listing 7-31 and Figure 7-33). The elements are disorganized, without a guide mark, and are visually compacted.

Listing 7-31. Lists for Grouping (ListGroups.html)

```
1   <ul class="list-group">
2     <li class="list-group-item">These options</li>
3     <li class="list-group-item">here</li>
4     <li class="list-group-item">for all users</li>
5     <li class="list-group-item">this application</li>
6     <li class="list-group-item">generally available</li>
7   </ul>
```

These options

here

for all users

this application

generally available

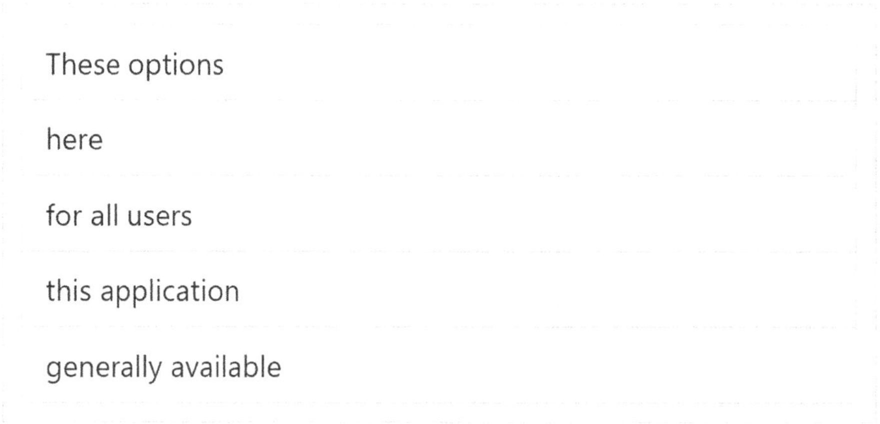

Figure 7-33. *Lists for grouping*

Badges in Lists

Badges can be placed in the text of the list items in lists at any point (see Listing 7-32 and Figure 7-34).

Listing 7-32. Lists with Tags (ListBadges.html)

```
1   <ul class="list-group">
2     <li class="list-group-item">
3       <span class="badge badge-primary">14</span>
4       Options
5     </li>
6     <li class="list-group-item">
7       <span class="badge badge-danger">7</span>
8       Application
9     </li>
10  </ul>
```

14 Options

7 Applications

Figure 7-34. *Lists with tags*

Links in Lists

You also can use hyperlinks in lists (see Listing 7-33). This practical approach makes more individualized menus that look similar, but behave differently.

Listing 7-33. Lists of Links (ListLinks.html)

```
1   <div class="list-group">
2     <a href="#" class="list-group-item active">
3       These options
4     </a>
5     <a href="#" class="list-group-item">are available</a>
```

```
6      <a href="#" class="list-group-item">to all users</a>
7      <a href="#" class="list-group-item">of this app</a>
8    </div>
```

This presentation looks very similar to buttons; only the function corresponds to a hyperlink (see Figure 7-35). You should be wary of these representations, because the behavior is not immediately apparent to the user.

Figure 7-35. *Lists of links*

Buttons in Lists

You can use buttons in lists (see Listing 7-34 and Figure 7-36). Unlike normal buttons, these are *not* based on the class *.btn*. They provide a frame, but are not colored on the entire surface as normal buttons are.

Listing 7-34. Lists with Buttons (ListBtns.html)

```
1    <div class="list-group">
2      <button type="button"
3                class="list-group-item list-group-item-success">
4        Option A
5      </button>
```

```
6     <button type="button"
7             class="list-group-item list-group-item-danger">
8       Option B
9     </button>
10    <button type="button"
11            class="list-group-item list-group-item-info">
12      Option C
13    </button>
14  </div>
```

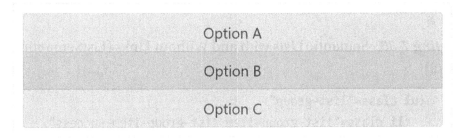

Figure 7-36. *Lists with buttons*

With the class *.disabled* within *.list-group-item*, the contents will appear disabled.

```
1   <div class="list-group">
2     <a href="#" class="list-group-item disabled">
3       These options
4     </a>
5     <a href="#" class="list-group-item">are here</a>
6     <a href="#" class="list-group-item">for all users</a>
7     <a href="#" class="list-group-item">this application</a>
8     <a href="#" class="list-group-item">generally
      available</a>
9   </div>
```

List elements can have a semantic meaning (see Listing 7-35 and Figure 7-37).

- *list-group-item-success*: success, green

- *list-group-item-info*: information, azure

- *list-group-item-warning*: warning, orange

- *list-group-item-danger*: danger, red

Active elements can also be highlighted with the *.active* class. The common nonsematic classes are also available (primary, secondary, light, dark).

Listing 7-35. Semantic Lists with and Without Links (ListSemantics. html)

```
1   <ul class="list-group">
2     <li class="list-group-item list-group-item-success">
3       Success
4     </li>
5     <li class="list-group-item list-group-item-info">
6       Info
7     </li>
8     <li class="list-group-item list-group-item-warning">
9       Warning
10    </li>
11    <li class="list-group-item list-group-item-danger">
12      Danger
13    </li>
14  </ul>
```

```
15   <div class="list-group">
16     <a href="#"
17        class="list-group-item list-group-item-success">
18       Success
19     </a>
20     <a href="#"
21        class="list-group-item list-group-item-info">
22       Info
23     </a>
24     <a href="#"
25        class="list-group-item list-group-item-warning">
26       Warning
27     </a>
28     <a href="#"
29        class="list-group-item list-group-item-danger">
30       Danger
31     </a>
32   </div>
```

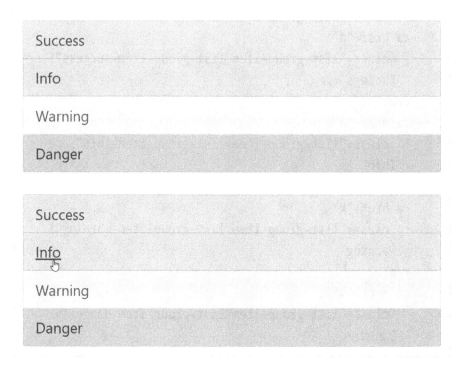

Figure 7-37. *Semantic lists with and without links*

The list elements themselves are very flexible and can include almost all of the other components, as shown in Listing 7-36 and Figure 7-38.

Listing 7-36. Lists with Headings (ListHeader.html)

```
1  <div class="list-group">
2    <a href="#" class="list-group-item active">
3      <h4 class="list-group-item-heading">Title</h4>
4      <p class="list-group-item-text">...</p>
5    </a>
6  </div>
```

Figure 7-38. *Lists with headings*

Cards

Cards are highlighted areas that serve to structure the page. These areas may have a semantic meaning. They are very diverse and serve a wide range of tasks. A minimalistic structure would look like this:

```
1   <div class="card card-body">
2     <div class="card-text">
3       Example text
4     </div>
5   </div>
```

Semantic and nonsemantic meaning is achieved with background classes (*.bg-<type>*).

The default panel appears as in Listing 7-37 and as shown in Figure 7-39.

Listing 7-37. Card (Cards_Danger.html)

```
1   <div class="card bg-danger text-light">
2   <div class="card-text">
3   Example text
4   </div>
5   </div>
```

Figure 7-39. *Card with class .card-danger*

Semantic variants have the same shape and change the color of the background, like buttons.

```
1   <div class="card bg-primary">...</div>
2   <div class="card bg-success">...</div>
3   <div class="card bg-info">...</div>
4   <div class="card bg-warning">...</div>
5   <div class="card bg-danger">...</div>
```

If the font color has an insufficient contrast, you can get a better representation using the class *.text-light*. This makes sense at least in *danger* class, where the font color changes for the dark red background from black to white.

The standard menu is preceded by *.card*. A general internal spacing (padding) is achieved with *.card-body*. The text is created in *.card-text*.

Headings

Cards can create complex reports and can include a header area. This part is preceded by *.card-header*. In the header, the size can be varied with <h1>-<h6>.

Listing 7-38 provides the default formatting of the heading, and Figure 7-40 shows a heading.

Listing 7-38. Card with Heading (Cards_Header.html)

```
1   <div class="card ">
2   <div class="card-header">Message</div>
3   <p class="card-body">
```

```
4    Message text
5    </p>
6    </div>
```

Message

Message text

Figure 7-40. *Card with heading*

To style headings, use a code that looks like the one in Listing 7-39 and shown in Figure 7-41.

Listing 7-39. Card with Title (Cards_Header2.html)

```
1    <div class="card ">
2    <h2 class="card-header">Message</h2>
3    <p class="card-body">
4    Message Text
5    </p>
6    </div>
```

Message

Message text

Figure 7-41. *Card with title and heading element*

It is also possible to place subheadings on *.card-subtitle*.

Footers

The footer areas of panels appear in *.card-footer*. The footer does not inherit semantic information, and it is up to you to add it here (see Listing 7-40 and Figure 7-42). Footers are for the placement of buttons, and these can bring their own semantic context, if necessary. Resulting actions are then programmed separately, as the footer provides no interactive elements.

Listing 7-40. Semantic Card with Footer (Cards_Footer.html)

```
1    <div class="card bg-success">
2    <p class="card-body">
3            This is the content...
4    </p>
5    <div class="card-footer">Footer</div>
6    </div>
```

Figure 7-42. *Semantic card with footer*

Cards with Tables

The card presentation of data provides tables for output, too. Note, however, that there are limited possibilities for responsive layouts with tables. Because cards already have a frame, tables should be drawn without them.

The placement may be made in *.card-text* or placed outside. If it is made within, the table should get additional distance, if space permits (see Listing 7-41 and Figure 7-43).

Listing 7-41. Card with Table (Excerpt from Cards_Table.html)

```
1    <div class="card">
2      <div class="card-header">Title</div>
3        <div class="card-body">
4        <p>...</p>
5      </div>
6
7      <!-- Table -->
8      <table class="table table-sm">
9        ...
10     </table>
11   </div>
```

Figure 7-43. *Card with table*

Within *.card-text* there is a seamless transition between content and table.

Cards with Lists

Lists can be simply placed in cards, as shown in Listing 7-42 and Figure 7-44.

Listing 7-42. Card with List (Cards_List.html)

```
1    <div class="card">
2      <div class="card-header">Knowledge</div>
3        <div class="card-body">
4          <ul class="list-group list-group-flush">
5            <li class="list-group-item">Bootstrap</li>
6            <li class="list-group-item">jQuery</li>
7            <li class="list-group-item">Angular</li>
8            <li class="list-group-item">React</li>
9            <li class="list-group-item">@nyaf</li>
10          </ul>
11        </div>
12      </div>
13    </div>
```

Knowledge

    Bootstrap

    jQuery

    Angular

    React

    @nyaf

Figure 7-44. *Card with list*

Card with Pictures

Images can be as simple as a map in the background (overlay). The superimposition of text is achieved by *.card-img-overlay* (see Listing 7-43 and Figure 7-45).

Listing 7-43.   Card with Background Image (Cards_Image.html)

```
1    <div class="card"
2         style="width: 300px">
3      <img class="card-img-top"
4           src="../Res/Background.jpg" alt="Lamp">
5      <div class="card-img-overlay card-inverse text-right">
6        <h4 class="card-title">Received?</h4>
7        <p class="card-text">This is Bootstrap 4</p>
8      </div>
9      <div class="card-body text-center">
10       Proceed with the new styles...
11     </div>
12   </div>
```

The image should be tailored to the width of the card, as shown in Listing 7-43 on line 2, to 300 px. Please note that such fixed values may not be responsive.

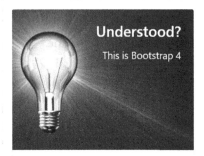

Proceed with the new styles...

Figure 7-45. *Card with background image*

There is the option to combine the width and the distance to the column classes for placement in the grid.

Additional functions for placing images are as follows:

- *.card-img-top*: aligning the image upward

- *.card-img-bottom*: aligning the image downward; these classes are directly applied to the <img /> tag.

Cards in the Grid

The last example demonstrates how the width can be adjusted directly by a style. Bootstrap has no explicit classes for this purpose. It is better to adjust the placement of the grid, as shown in Listing 7-44 and Figure 7-46.

Listing 7-44. Cards in the Grid (Cards_Grid.html)

```
1    <div class="container-fluid sample">
2      <div class="row">
3        <div class="col-6">
4          <div class="card card-success">
```

```
 5          <div class="card-body bg-success text-light">
 6          <h4 class="card-title">Message</h4>
 7          <p class="card-text">
 8            This action was successful.
 9          </p>
10          <a href="#" class="card-link">
11            More...
12          </a>
13          <a href="#" class="card-link">
14            Back...
15          </a>
16        </div>
17      </div>
18    </div>
19    <div class="col-6">
20        <div class="card bg-warning">
21          <div class="card-body">
22            <h4 class="card-title">Message</h4>
23            <p class="card-text">
24              Something went wrong.
25            </p>
26            <a href="#" class="btn btn-danger">
27              Exception...
28            </a>
29          </div>
30        </div>
31      </div>
32    </div>
33  </div>
```

Figure 7-46. *Cards in the grid*

Deck of Cards

Cards can be arranged horizontally so that all the elements have the same height (see Listing 7-45 and Figure 7-47).

Listing 7-45. Align Cards (Cards_Deck.html)

```
1   <div class="container-fluid sample">
2     <div class="card-deck-wrapper">
3       <div class="card-deck">
4       <!-- Card 1 -->
5       <div class="card">
6         <div class="card-header">Help 1</div>
7           <div class="card-body">
8             <p class="card-text">Help text.</p>
9           </div>
10        </div>
11      <!-- Card 2 -->
12      <div class="card">
13        <div class="card-header">Help 2</div>
14          <div class="card-body">
15            <p class="card-text">Help text and
16              <a href="#" class="card-link">more help</a>.
17            </p>
```

```
18            <p class="card-text">This is more text than in
              the first box</p>
19          </div>
20        </div>
21      </div>
22    </div>
23  </div>
```

Help 1	Help 2
Help text.	Help text and more help.
	This is more text than in the first box

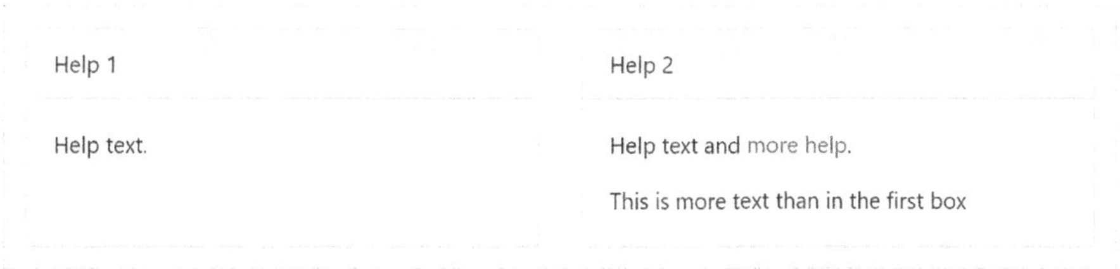

Figure 7-47. *Align cards*

Card Groups

Cards can be horizontally arranged so that all the elements have the same height. The groups are directly connected to each other (as opposed to the stack). For this purpose, the card group is packaged in a class *.card-group* (see Listing 7-46 and Figure 7-48).

Listing 7-46. Card Group (Cards_Group.html)

```
1  <div class="card-group">
2  <!-- Card 1 -->
3  <div class="card bg-success">
4  <div class="card-header">Info</div>
5  <div class="card-body">
6  <p class="card-text">Info text here</p>
7  </div>
8  </div>
```

```
 9   <!-- Card 2 -->
10   <div class="card bg-info">
11   <div class="card-header">Message</div>
12   <div class="card-body">
13   <p class="card-text">here comes more...</p>
14   </div>
15   </div>
16   </div>
```

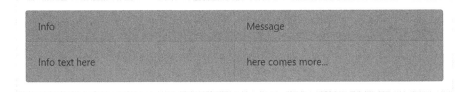

Figure 7-48. *Card group*

Note   The horizontal alignment may be connected to the column layout, so that you also can control the width.

Cards in Columns

Cards can be distributed horizontally in columns, so that complex layouts with dedicated designs of blocks are possible. For this purpose, the card group is packaged in a class *.card-columns* (see Listing 7-47 and Figure 7-49).

Listing 7-47. Card Columns (Cards_Columns.html)

```
1   <div class="container sample">
2   <div class="row">
3   <div class="card-columns">
4   <!-- Card 1 -->
5   <div class="card">
```

```
 6    <div class="card-header">Card 1</div>
 7    <div class="card-body">
 8    <p class="card-text">This is the content.</p>
 9    </div>
10    </div>
11    <!-- Card 2 -->
12    <div class="card">
13    <div class="card- body ">
14    <h4 class="card-title">Card 2</h4>
15    <p class="card-text">This is the content.</p>
16    </div>
17    </div>
18    <!-- Card 3 -->
19    <div class="card border-info">
20    <div class="card-header">Card 3</div>
21    <div class="card- body bg-info">
22    <p class="card-text">
23    Here is the content.
24    A <a href="#" class="card-link">Link</a>.
25    </p>
26    </div>
27    <div class="card-footer">Footer</div>
28    </div>
29    <!-- Card 4 -->
30    <div class="card card-outline-warning">
31    <div class="card-header">Card 4</div>
32    <div class="card-body bg-warning">
33    <p class="card-text">This is the content.</p>
34    </div>
35    <div class="card-footer">Footer</div>
36    </div>
37    <!-- Card 5 -->
```

```
38   <div class="card">
39   <div class="card-body ">
40   <h4 class="card-title">Card 5</h4>
41   <p class="card-text">This is the content.</p>
42   </div>
43   </div>
44   <!-- Card 6 -->
45   <div class="card border-success">
46   <div class="card-header">Card 6</div>
47   <div class="card-body bg-success">
48   <p class="card-text"> 49              Here is the content.
49   A <a href="#" class="card-link">Link</a>.
50   </p>
51   </div>
52   </div>
53   <!-- Card 7 -->
54   <div class="card">
55   <div class="card-header">Card 7</div>
56   <div class="card-body">
57   <p class="card-text">
58   Here is the content
59   A <a href="#" class="card-link">Link</a>.
60   </p>
61   </div>
62   <div class="card-footer">End</div>
63   </div>
64   <!-- Cars 8 -->
65   <div class="card">
66   <div class="card-body">
67   <h4 class="card-title">Card 8</h4>
68   <p class="card-text">Here is the content.</p>
69   </div>
```

```
70    </div>
71    </div>
72    </div>
73    </div>
```

In this example the semantic classes *.card-outline-<>* is used to assign the color to the border only. This replaces the regular *.card-<>* classes that give cards a semantic meaning.

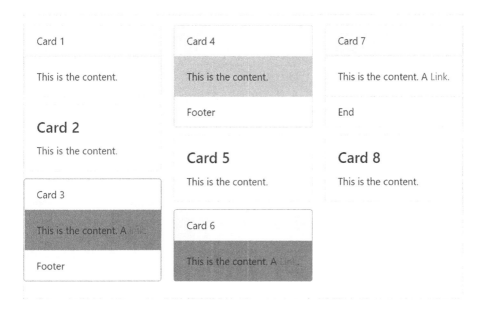

Figure 7-49. *Card columns*

Summary

This chapter provided an overview of layout components used to create the essential visual parts of an application. This includes important design elements such as navigation, message boxes, and buttons. The card component is another piece that is very universal and can be used to further structure your pages.

CHAPTER 8

Active Components

Active components in Bootstrap are written in and supported by JavaScript. This includes some programming interfaces to work with. Technically these are jQuery plug-ins. If the entire Bootstrap library is not used, it is possible to load only those parts that are really needed.

Setup and Activation

The files *bootstrap.js* and *bootstrap.min.js* (the minimized version) already contain all the components. To use this you also need to load jQuery. To use the components there are two options: either you use the HTML5 attributes beginning with data- or the JavaScript API. For the purposes of modern HTML5 programming, using attributes is preferred because it needs less script code, and thus there is less risk of making mistakes when programming.

The use of HTML5 attributes may occasionally be inappropriate or interferes with other modules of an application that uses the very same attributes. If so, it is possible to disable them globally (note the dot at the beginning of the name

```
1    $(document).off('.data-api')
```

If only a single plug-in is affected, you also can disable just that plug-in:

```
1    $(document).off('.alert.data-api')
```

© Jörg Krause 2020
J. Krause, *Introducing Bootstrap 4*, https://doi.org/10.1007/978-1-4842-6203-0_8

In more complex scenarios, there is often the temptation to use multiple plug-ins with a component. This will not work. Imagine a button that activates a modal dialog and simultaneously displays a tooltip. Although this may be useful in design, it will not work. This can be achieved simply with another enclosing member. The outer member—without frames and distances—controls the tooltip and the inner one the modal dialog.

Javascript Frameworks   There are several frameworks for web site programming, such as Angular, React, or Vue. Some competing UI libraries exist, such as jQuery UI. Although jQuery is the basis of Bootstrap components, these frameworks compete with Bootstrap and should not be used simultaneously under any circumstances. Often you can find a compatibility library that handles the conflicts (for example,with Angular you may use **ngBootstrap** instead of Bootstrap, and have the same components but in Angular style).

The Programming Interface

With web sites created entirely in JavaScript, which is quite common nowadays, there are limited possibilities using the attributes to control the behavior. The typical way to work with the API is using the jQuery programming style, like this:

```
1   $('.btn.danger').button('toggle').addClass('fat');
```

The leading $ sign is a function call (JavaScript allows the $ literal as a name). That call queries the page for the given selector, which follows CSS rules. It returns another jQuery instance, so you can immediately execute functions on the selected elements. Like the functions delivered with jQuery, Bootstrap adds more such calls for the components described in this chapter.

All components process an *Options* object that needs to be provided as an anonymous object. The actual values are dependent on the component. See a example here using the function "model," which creates a modal dialog.

```
1   $('#myModal').modal()                        // Only Standard
2   $('#myModal').modal({ keyboard: false })     // With Option
3   $('#myModal').modal('show')                  // Trigger action
```

Each component has a constructor. This example uses the component "popover"_:

```
1   $.fn.popover.Constructor
```

The constructor returns a property DEFAULTS objects that allows access to the default values. This is helpful to change the behavior globally or to reset settings.

```
1   $.fn.modal.Constructor.DEFAULTS.keyboard = false;
```

Note   The leading $.fn. is the access to registered plug-ins in jQuery. This part is not specific to Bootstrap, but is a requirement of jQuery.

A specific instance can be obtained as follows:

```
1   $('[rel="popover"]').data('popover'');
```

This is an example of a "popover."

Conflict Prevention

If jQuery is still used in addition to other libraries or jQuery plug-ins, it may lead to name conflicts. As JavaScript does not have namespaces, you may need to do this manually. This is the purpose of the method noConflict.

```
1    var bootstrapButton = $.fn.button.noConflict();
2    $.fn.bootstrapBtn = bootstrapButton;
```

In line 1, an instance of the plug-in is retrieved. This is then assigned a new name in line 2, which does not interfere with other elements.

In this context, versions are important. These can be retrieved with VERSION:

```
1    $.fn.tooltip.Constructor.VERSION // => "4.0.0"
```

Events

Bootstrap components generate some private events. Most of these are available in two versions—the occurrence of the event and the end of processing. Accordingly, the verbs are available: basic and past tense ("show" and "shown"). All events are in their own namespaces ".bs.".

As some events are handled internally, you can suppress them by *preventDefault*. This is the typical way for jQuery.

```
1    $('#myModal').on('show.bs.modal', function (e) {
2    if (!data) return e.preventDefault() 3    })
```

Here the code in line 2 prevents the standard behavior. The modal dialog, which actually appears in "show," is suppressed. Of course, only events that currently occur can be suppressed, such as "show." If the event has been completed, as in "shown," there is no longer such an option.

Transitions

Transitions are largely covered by CSS3. To support older browsers, there are covered by the auxiliary library *transitions.js*, mapping the effects in JavaScript. This library is part of *bootstrap.js* and does not need to be installed separately. This is only necessary when parts of the library are used.

Transition effects can be bothersome. Therefore, they can be switched off globally:

```
1   $.support.transition = false
```

Note   Animations—whether as direct effect or transition—are only amusing the first time. Omit them, and users benefit.

Applications of the module include things such as:

- Dialogues are gently faded in and out.

- Switching between tabs is changed gently.

- Messages can be smoothly displayed.

- The Carousel has replaced its content with animation.

The effect is triggered by the class *.fade*.

Modal Dialogs

Modal dialogs are from *modals.js*. This library is part of *bootstrap.js* and does not need to be installed separately.

Features

Modal dialogs seize exclusive focus and demand an unconditional response from the user. You should never use modal dialogs without the possibility of interaction. A button or an icon for closing is always required.

A modal dialog is exclusive, so only one dialog at a time can be open.

Normally you should place modal dialogs on top of the page. This prevents conflicts with other settings. When and where they are called, however, is completely independent.

On mobile devices, it could be that the first element of the dialogue is not in focus, even if the attribute autofocus is used. If necessary, you can use a little JavaScript to post help:

```
1    $('#myModal').on('shown.bs.modal', function () {
2    $('#myInput').focus()
3    })
```

A standard dialog consists of three parts:

- Header area

- Content

- Footer area

The title comes in the header area, the contents then fills the dialogue, and action buttons are placed in the footer, as shown in Listing 8-1:

Listing 8-1. Modal Dialog (Modal.html)

```
1    <div class="modal fade" id="myModal">
2    <div class="modal-dialog">
3        <div class="modal-content">
4          <div class="modal-header">
5            <h4 class="modal-title">Title</h4>
6              <button type="button" class="close"
```

```
 7                       data-dismiss="modal"
 8                       aria-label="Close">
 9               <span aria-hidden="true">&times;</span>
10               </button>
11          </div>
12          <div class="modal-body">
13            <p>The content &hellip;</p>
14          </div>
15          <div class="modal-footer">
16              <button type="button" class="btn btn-default"
17                       data-dismiss="modal">Close</button>
18              <button type="button" class="btn btn-primary">
19               Save
20              </button>
21          </div>
22        </div>
23      </div>
24    </div>
```

To display the dialog, an action on the page is required. This may look like Listing 8-2 and Figure 8-1:

Listing 8-2. Trigger for Dialogue (Modal.html)

```
1   <button type="button" class="btn btn-primary btn-lg"
2           data-toggle="modal"
3           data-target="#myModal">
4         Show Dialog
5   </button>
```

Figure 8-1. *Modal dialog*

As with previous examples, a barrier-free access is recommended. First take the attributes role="dialog" and aria-labelledby="..."; the latter should point to an element that contains the title. As the dialogue itself, the contents are decorated with role="document." If a description is required, which may not appear useful in normal operation because the dialogue is in a context or contains images and symbols, use the more descriptive aria-describedby on the element with the class *.modal*.

Dialog Sizes

Modal dialogs have three sizes, which are set by two classes (shown in Listing 8-3 and Listing 8-4):

- *.bs-example-modal-lg*: greater than normal

- *.bs-example-modal-sm*: smaller than normal

Listing 8-3. A .bs-example-modal-lg Example

```
1   <button type="button" class="btn btn-primary"
2           data-toggle="modal"
3           data-target=".bs-example-modal-lg">
4       Big dialogue
5   </button>
6
```

```
7    <div class="modal fade bs-example-modal-lg"
8          tabindex="-1"
9          role="dialog"
10         aria-labelledby="myLargeModalLabel">
11      <div class="modal-dialog modal-lg">
12        <div class="modal-content">
13        ...
14        </div>
15      </div>
16    </div>
```

Listing 8-4. A .bs-example-modal-sm Example

```
1    <button type="button" class="btn btn-primary"
2            data-toggle="modal"
3            data-target=".bs-example-modal-sm">Small</button>
4
5    <div class="modal fade bs-example-modal-sm"
6        tabindex="-1"
7        role="dialog"
8        aria-labelledby="mySmallModalLabel">
9      <div class="modal-dialog modal-sm">
10        <div class="modal-content">
11        ...
12        </div>
13      </div>
14    </div>
```

Animations are created with *.fade.* This can be annoying, and should not be used on mobile devices.

Note   The effect of fading requires significant processing power and reduces the battery life in mobile devices

---

Dialog with Grid

Dialogs can be extensive, and can therefore benefit from grids. To achieve this the body (*.modal-body*) of the dialog gets a new container *.container-fluid* within. In this container, the normal grid classes are applicable. The outer width depends on the width of the dialog, and the values are in percentage terms (see Listing 8-5 and Figure 8-2).

Listing 8-5.   Complex Dialogue with Grid (Modal_Complex.html)

```
 1   <div class="modal fade" role="dialog" id="myModal"
 2        aria-labelledby="gridSystemModalLabel">
 3     <div class="modal-dialog" role="document">
 4       <div class="modal-content">
 5         <div class="modal-header">
 6           <h4 class="modal-title"
 7                id="gridSystemModalLabel">Title</h4>
 8           <button type="button" class="close"
 9                   data-dismiss="modal"
10                   aria-label="Close">
11             <span aria-hidden="true">&times;</span>
12           </button>
13         </div>
14         <div class="modal-body">
15           <div class="container-fluid">
16             <div class="row">
17               <div class="col-md-4">4</div>
```

```
18              <div class="col-md-4 offset-md-4">4 4</div>
19            </div>
20            <div class="row">
21              <div class="col-md-3 offset-md-3">3 3</div>
22              <div class="col-md-2 offset-md-4">2 4</div>
23            </div>
24            <div class="row">
25              <div class="col-md-6 offset-md-3">6 3</div>
26            </div>
27            <div class="row">
28              <div class="col-sm-9">
29              Level 1: .col-sm-9
30              </div>
31            </div>
32            <div class="row">
33              <div class="col-sm-8 col-md-6">
34               Level 2: .col-sm-8 .col-md-6
35              </div>
36              <div class="col-sm-4 col-md-6">
37               Level 2: .col-sm-4 .col-md-6
38              </div>
39            </div>
40          </div>
41        </div>
42      </div>
43    </div>
44    <div class="modal-footer">
45     <button type="button"
46            class="btn btn-secondary"
47            data-dismiss="modal">
48        Close
49     </button>
```

```
50        <button type="button"
51                 class="btn btn-primary">
52            Save
53        </button>
54      </div>
55     </div>
56    </div>
57   </div>
58   <div class="container sample">
59    <button type="button"
60             class="btn btn-primary btn-lg"
61             data-toggle="modal"
62             data-target="#myModal">
63           Show dialog
64    </button>
65   </div>
```

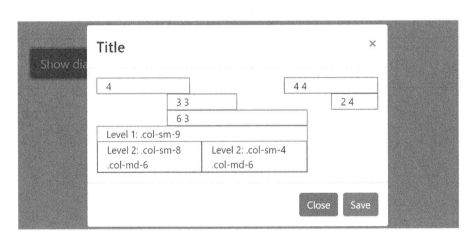

Figure 8-2. *Using the grid withing a dialog*

The button or action that triggers the dialogue is initiated and can transmit more values to modify the dialog. Listing 8-6 shows how this is accomplished by data-attributes.

Listing 8-6. Controlled Dialog (Modal_Data.html)

```
1    <button type="button" class="btn btn-primary"
2            data-toggle="modal"
3            data-target="#exampleModal"
4            data-whatever="anna@muster.de">
5       Open Anna
6    </button>
7    <button type="button" class="btn btn-primary"
8            data-toggle="modal"
9            data-target="#exampleModal"
10           data-whatever="berta@muster.de">
11      Open Berta
12   </button>
13   <button type="button" class="btn btn-primary"
14           data-toggle="modal"
15           data-target="#exampleModal"
16           data-whatever="chri@muster.de">
17      Open Chris
18   </button>
19
20   <div class="modal fade" id="exampleModal" tabindex="-1"
21        role="dialog" aria-labelledby="exampleModalLabel">
22     <div class="modal-dialog" role="document">
23       <div class="modal-content">
24         <div class="modal-header">
25           <h4 class="modal-title" id="exampleModalLabel">
26             New message
27           </h4>
```

```
28        <button type="button" class="close"
29                data-dismiss="modal"
30                aria-label="Close">
31       <span aria-hidden="true">&times;</span>
32       </button>
33      </div>
34      <div class="modal-body">
35      <form>
36        <div class="form-group">
37          <label for="recipient" class="control-label">
38           Receiver:
39          </label>
40          <input type="text" class="form-control"
41                id="recipient">
42        </div>
43        <div class="form-group">
44          <label for="message-text" class="control-label">
45            Message:
46          </label>
47          <textarea class="form-control"
48                    id="message-text">
49          </textarea>
50        </div>
51      </form>
52      </div>
53      <div class="modal-footer">
54        <button type="button" class="btn btn-default"
55                data-dismiss="modal">
56        Conclude
57        </button>
```

```
58        <button type="button" class="btn btn-primary">
59          Send
60        </button>
61      </div>
62    </div>
63    </div>
64  </div>
```

The evaluation then takes some JavaScript, as follows:

```
1   $(function() {
2     $('#exampleModal').on('show.bs.modal', function(event) {
3       var button = $(event.relatedTarget);
4       var recipient = button.data('whatever');
5       var modal = $(this);
6       modal.find('.modal-title')
7             .text('Message' + recipient);
8       modal.find('#Recipient').val(recipient);
9     });
10  });
```

In line 2, the button is determined. In line 3 the private attribute data-whatever is accessed to copy the data in the dialog. This is the easiest way via the DOM of dialogue (see Figure 8-3).

Figure 8-3. *Controlled dialog*

General Information About Behavior

Modal dialogs will give the page a slightly opaque look, to catch the attention of the user. That is done internally by adding the class *.modal- open* to the body element. You can give to this class more styles to customize the effect. Agent *.modal-backdrop* used another class that ensures that the dialog will be closed when the user clicks outside (despair click).

The trigger behavior is based on attributes:

- `data-toggle="modal"`: trigger, for example, on a button

- `data-target="#foo"`: target for dialogue *#foo*

- `href="#foo"`: alternative specifying the destination for dialog *#foo*

- id="foo": decoration of the dialogue itself (destination ID)

```
1   <button type="button"
2            data-toggle="modal"
3            data-target="#myModal">
4      Show Modal
5   </button>
```

In JavaScript, the selectors of jQuery are used:

```
1   $('#myModal').modal(options)
```

Options

Options may be set as a data-attribute in HTML or with code. The suffix of the data-attribute corresponds to the name of the property. Table 8-1 lists options, Table 8-2 lists actions, and Table 8-3 lists events for modal dialogs.

Table 8-1. *Options for Modal Dialogs*

Name	Type	Description
backdrop	Boolean or "static"	True will close when clicking outside; "static" suppresses closing
keyboard	Boolean	Closes the dialog when ESC is pressed
show	Boolean	Instant display during initialization
focus	Boolean	Moves focus (caret position) to the dialog

Table 8-2. *Actions for Modal Dialogs*

Name	Description
show	Dialog appears
toggle	Toggle display state asynchronously
hide	Close
handleUpdate	Repositions by moving or showing the scrollbar
dispose	Destroys the element

Table 8-3. *Events for Modal Dialogs*

Name	Description
show.bs.modal	Dialog appears
hide.bs.modal	Dialog closing
shown.bs.modal	Appears (on transitions, and animations will be serviced)
hidden.bs.modal	Has been closed (on transitions, and animations will be serviced)
loaded.bs.modal	Is loaded
hidePrevented. bs.modal	If the dialog is already open, the backdrop is "static" and the user clicks outside (or hits ESC), this event fires; usage is to prevent closing the dialog

Using the Options

The calls to your code look like this:

```
1   .modal(options)
```

The complete code based on HTML code with the ID *myModal* might look like this:

```
1   $('#myModal').modal('show')
```

Please read the following fluent syntax on line 4, which will be continued with the object to trigger further actions.

```
1   $('#myModal').modal({
2     keyboard: false
3   })
4   .modal('toggle')
```

For events to respond add the callback function:

```
1   $('#myModal').on('hidden.bs.modal', function (e) {
2     // Event code...});
```

Pull-Down Menu (Drop-Down)

The drop-down menu is available in a simple form without JavaScript support (already covered in Chapter 7). The possible interactions enhance the function of navigation bar (navbar), tabs, and pills. For more advanced scenarios, additional coding effort is required.

Common Information About Behavior

Show invisible elements dynamically and again hide can be carried out by turning on and off the class *.open*. On mobile devices *.dropdown-backdrop* will work for the whole screen and "tap" for the event. That is, it does not automatically close the menu on such devices, but must be closed with extra finger pressure before another menu item can be selected.

Note   The attribute data-toggle="dropdown" is always required.

Options

The pull-down menu has several options, mostly derived from the popper. js library that provides the functionality (shown in Table 8-4). For a more detailed description visit the Popper.js website.[1]

Table 8-4. *Actions for Drop Menus*

Name	Description
offset	Move the drop-down using a pixel value or a callback function
flip	Flip if the drop-down overlaps the element (default behavior)
boundary	Control the overflow with "viewport," "window," "scrollParent," or an HTMLElement reference
reference	Use "toggle" or "parent" or an HTMLElement reference to access the drop-down element
display	Use "dynamic" or "static" for positioning
popperConfig	Configure the underlying popper.js library

See Table 8-5 for actions and Table 8-6 for events for drop menus.

---

[1]Popper.Defaults, `https://popper.js.org/docs/v1/#Popper.Defaults`.

Table 8-5. *Actions for Drop Menus*

Name	Description
toggle	Display state changes to opposite
show	Show the drop-down part
hide	Hide the drop-down part
update	Update the position; necessary if the surrounding elements change their position and the drop-down button moves up or down, in which case a formerly positioned menu would stay at the last position
dispose	Destroy the element's drop-down

Table 8-6. *Events for Drop Menus*

Name	Description
show.bs.dropdown	Show
hide.bs.dropdown	Close
shown.bs.dropdown	Display was (on transitions and animations will be serviced)
hidden.bs.dropdown	Has been closed (on transitions and animations will be serviced)
loaded.bs.dropdown	Is loaded

Using the Options

Based on the code of the static folding, the HTML menu is practically identical:

```
1    <div class="dropdown">
2      <button id="dLabel" type="button"
3              data-toggle="dropdown"
4              aria-haspopup="true" aria-expanded="false">
```

```
5          Trigger drop
6          <span class="caret"></span>
7      </button>
8      <ul class="dropdown-menu" aria-labelledby="dLabel">
9          ...
10     </ul>
11   </div>
```

Hyperlinks are used and instead of the href-attribute, you use data-target instead of href="#."

```
1    <div class="dropdown">
2      <a id="dLabel" data-target="#"
3         href="http://example.com"
4         data-toggle="dropdown" role="button"
5         aria-haspopup="true" aria-expanded="false">
6       Trigger drop
7       <span class="caret"></span>
8      </a>
9      <ul class="dropdown-menu"
     aria-labelledby="dLabel">
10         ...
11     </ul>
12   </div>
```

The code to use is as follows:

```
1    $('.dropdown-toggle').dropdown()
```

For events to respond you add the callback function:

```
1    $('#myDropdown').on('show.bs.dropdown', function () {
2      // Do something...
3    })
```

Scroll Bar Supervisor (ScrollSpy)

This component recognizes the position of the scroll bar. The jump destinations can be dependent on the update position of the scroll bar in a navigation bar. This is especially interesting for very long pages, where the jump destinations in a list of hyperlinks at the side are left or right and above that are always visible. When the user clicks on a link, the page jumps to the target position. This is normal browser behavior. However, if the scroll bar is used, a certain position sometimes appears. With *Scrollbar-supervisor* the menu is then suitably adjusted to the position so that the current visible section is highlighted. For the menu to display this effect, it must remain visible while scrolling. The purpose should be tacking navigation. This can be achieved with position: sticky. The affix component from Bootstrap 3 no longer exists.

Features

First, a navigation component is needed. The resolution of the jump destinations must be done on *id*. An object that was created with `<a href="#home">home</a>` must lead to a matching `<div id="home"></div>`. Invisible elements are ignored. The criterion for visibility applies, when jQuery uses the pseudoselectors: `:visible` indicators. This monitors the scroll area of an element. It needs `position:relative` to be positioned. This is usually `<body>` and there is no further action required. It is another element that also must accommodate overflow: scroll and a height must also be specified.

The activation is done with data-spy="scroll" on the monitored element, such as <body>. Data-target is then put on the *id* or class of the parent element of a component *.nav* that was used to start.

```
1    <style>
2    body {
3    position: relative;
4    }
5    </style>
6
7     <body data-spy="scroll" data-target="#navbar-example">
8        ...
9    <div id="navbar-example">
10   <ul class="nav nav-tabs" role="tablist">
11         ...
12   </ul>
13   </div>
14     ...
15   </body>
```

When using JavaScript, it looks like this:

```
1    $('body').scrollspy({ target: '#navbar-example' })
```

If elements are dynamically added, they must explicitly call *'refresh'*.

```
1    $('[data-spy="scroll"]').each(function () {
2    var $spy = $(this).scrollspy('refresh')
3       })
```

For using events to only respond to user action, just add the callback function:

```
1    $('#myScrollspy').on('activate.bs.scrollspy', function () {
2      // tu was...
3    })
```

Options

Options may be set as a data--attributes in HTML or with code.

The suffix of the "data-"-attributes corresponds to the name of the property. Table 8-7 lists the options, Table 8-8 lists the actions, and Table 8-9 lists the events for (*ScrollbarSpy*).

Table 8-7. *Options for (ScrollbarSpy)*

Name	Type	Description
offset	Number	Distance from the top, is responsive to the appearance of the target elements; default value is 10 pixels
method	String	Finds the spied section; can be "auto," "offset," or "position."
target	Element	The element the scrollspy is applied; can be any form jQuery accepts (string, jQuery object, DOM element)

Table 8-8. *Action for (ScrollbarSpy)*

Name	Description
refresh	Synchronizes dynamic elements

Table 8-9. *Events for (ScrollbarSpy)*

Name	Description
activate.bs.scrollspy	Activated

Reversible Tabs (Tab)

Reversible tabulators can be modified by other elements. This is only supported on one level, and not for nested elements. This is the active part of the navigation element made with the *.nav-tabs* class described in Chapter 7. The purpose is to control the content of a tab in addition to the tab's navigational items.

Features

The activation in JavaScript looks like this:

```
1    $('#myTabs a').click(function (e) {
2    e.preventDefault()
3    $(this).tab('show')
4       })
```

The activation can be carried out flexibly by means of selectors:

```
1    $('#myTabs a[href="#profile"]').tab('show')
2    $('#myTabs a:first').tab('show')
3    $('#myTabs a:last').tab('show')
4    $('#myTabs li:eq(2) a').tab('show')
```

The code in line 1 uses a name; line 2 selects the first tab, line 3 the last. Line 4 is the third (2, that is, the value is 0-based) selected.

The attribute data-toggle="tab" or data-toggle="pill" does this in the markup (see Listing 8-7).

Listing 8-7. Interactive Tabs

```
1   <div>
2
3     <!-- Nav tabs -->
4       <ul class="nav nav-tabs" role="tablist">
5         <li role="presentation" class="active">
6           <a href="#home" aria-controls="home"
7              role="tab" data-toggle="tab">Home</a>
8         </li>
9         <li role="presentation">
10          <a href="#profile" aria-controls="profile"
11             role="tab" data-toggle="tab">Profile</a>
12        </li>
13        <li role="presentation">
14          <a href="#messages" aria-controls="messages"
15             role="tab" data-toggle="tab">Messages</a>
16        </li>
17        <li role="presentation">
18          <a href="#settings" aria-controls="settings"
19             role="tab" data-toggle="tab">Settings</a>
20        </li>
21      </ul>
22
23  <!-- Tab-content -->
24  <div class="tab-content">
25    <div role="tabpanel" class="tab-pane active" id="Home">
26  ...
27    </div>
28    <div role="tabpanel" class="tab-pane" id="Profile">
29    ...
30    </div>
```

```
31      <div role="tabpanel" class="tab-pane" id="Messages">
32      ...
33      </div>
34      <div role="tabpanel" class="tab-pane" id="Settings">
35          ...
36      </div>
37    </div>
38
39  </div>
```

For events to only respond, add the callback function:

```
1   $('a[data-toggle="tab"]').on('shown.bs.tab',
2       function (e) {
3           e.target // New Tab
4           e.relatedTarget // Previous Tab
5   })
```

Options

Options may be set as a data-attributes in HTML or with code. The suffix of the data-attributes corresponds to the name of the property. Table 8-10 lists the actions, and Table 8-11 lists the events for *Tabs*.

Table 8-10. *Actions for Tabs*

Name	Description
show	Shows the component
dispose	Destroys the component

Note that there is no "hide," because one tab is always active. If one is enabled, all others are hidden.

Table 8-11. *Events for Tabs*

Name	Description
hide.bs.tab	Tab is hidden
show.bs.tab	Tab is shown
hidden.bs.tab	Tab was hidden (by animation)
shown.bs.tab	Tab has been displayed (after animation)

Tooltip

Tooltips serve to provide useful information for the user (see Listing 8-8). They respond to a floating (hovering) mouse. Because showing many tooltips is critical to the performance of the browser they must be self-activated—the attributes alone are not enough.

Features

The tooltips require an additional library, "popper.js." There are also different styles available. See Listing 8-8 and Figure 8-4.

Listing 8-8. Tooltips for Buttons (Tooltip.html)

```
1    <button type="button" class="btn btn-primary"
2            data-toggle="tooltip" data-placement="left"
3            title="Tooltip on left">Tooltip left</button>
4
```

```
5    <button type="button" class="btn btn-primary "
6            data-toggle="tooltip" data-placement="top"
7            title="Tooltip on top">Tooltip top</button>
8
9    <button type="button" class="btn btn-primary "
10            data-toggle="tooltip" data-placement="bottom"
11            title="Tooltip on bottom">Tooltip bottom</button>
12
13    <button type="button" class="btn btn-primary "
14            data-toggle="tooltip" data-placement="right"
15            title="Tooltip on right">Tooltip right</button>
```

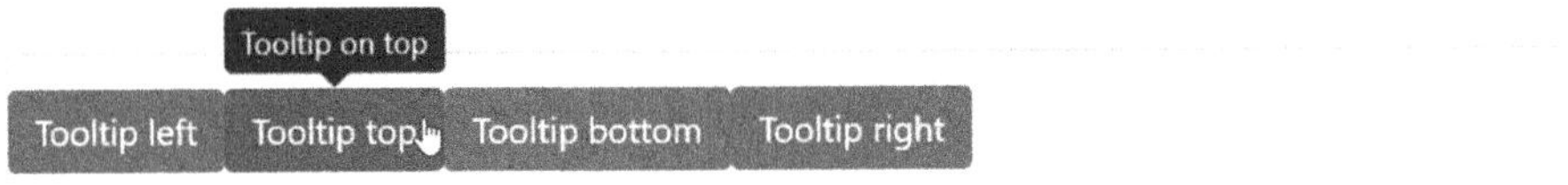

Figure 8-4. *The tooltip in action*

The activation always takes place in the script code. The following code activates all tooltips when the page loads.

```
1    $(function () {
2      $('[data-toggle="tooltip"]').tooltip()
3    })
```

For a tooltip that looks like this:

```
1    $('#example').tooltip(options)
```

The right to markup could be written as follows:

```
1    <a href="#" data-toggle="tooltip"
2      title="A tip will appear!"> Levitate mouse</a>
```

The markup generated is as follows:

```
1   <div class="tooltip top" role="tooltip">
2     <div class="tooltip-arrow"></div>
3       <div class="tooltip-inner">
4         A tip will appear!
5       </div>
6     </div>
7   </div>
```

Multiline Links

Sometimes the tips are somewhat more complex and have multiple lines. Normally, the text will automatically wrap and center. With white-space: nowrap; this upheaval is prevented. If such a tip in groups of buttons (with *.btn-group* or *.input-group*) is used, further measures are needed. In JavaScript, the container must be specified where the generated code is implanted in the DOM. In most, container: 'body' is sufficient.

General Tips

Tooltips for invisible elements are not a good idea. The tip will not be correctly placed, because the position of the reference element cannot be determined. View the reference element only and release the tooltip after its parent element becomes visible.

Otherwise, tooltips should only be used if the elements are being triggered by keystrokes. This can be achieved if you are limited to input elements. If this is not possible, use the attribute tabindex for an item to make it explicitly accessible.

If tooltips are visible on the deactivated elements, a wrapper must be built. It is best to add another <div> element and start the tooltip from there.

```
1   $('#myTooltip').on('hidden.bs.tooltip', function () {
2     // Do something...
3   })
```

Options

Options may be set as a data-attributes in HTML or with code. The suffix of the data-attributes corresponds to the name of the property. Table 8-12 lists the options, Table 8-13 lists the actions, and Table 8-14 lists the events for tooltips.

Table 8-12. Options for Tooltips

Name	Type	Description
animation	Boolean	Animation on the appearance
container	string or false	Positioning in another element
delay	number, object	Delay in milliseconds (default: 0), can also be an object { "show": 10, "hide": 10 }, then apply for the ads and hide different values
html	Boolean	HTML is allowed in the text
placement	string, function	Place the tip using "top," "bottom," "left," "right," and "auto" place so that the tooltip is always shown; for a function, they are determined by position itself

(continued)

Table 8-12. (*continued*)

Name	Type	Description
selector	String	To select the destination as a selector
template	String	Template in HTML
title	String	Content (text) of tooltips
trigger	String	Trigger: click, hover, focus, manual. Standard: "hover focus"
viewport	String, object, function	Standard: { selector: 'body', padding: 0 } or a selector or a selection function

The default template of the tooltip is as follows:

```
1   <div class="tooltip" role="tooltip">
2     <div class="tooltip-arrow"></div>
3     <div class="tooltip-inner"></div>
4   </div>
```

The text appears in *.tooltip-inner*.

Table 8-13. *Action for Tooltips*

Name	Description
show	Show
hide	Hide
toggle	Change from show to hide or vice versa
dispose	Destroy the component

Table 8-14. *Events for Tooltips*

Name	Description
hide.bs.tooltip	Tooltip is about to hide
show.bs.tooltip	Tooltip is about to show
hidden.bs.tooltip	Tooltip is hidden (by animation)
shown.bs.tooltip	Tooltip is shown (after animation)
inserted.bs.tooltip	

Content Overlay (Popover)

The somewhat cumbersome term content overlay (popover) represents a brief appearance, but not a modal dialog, usually without interaction. The most important applications are for giving detailed help. This is always appropriate when tooltips are no longer sufficient. Because many overlays are critical to the performance of the browser, they must be explicitly enabled; the attributes alone are not enough.

Content overlays can be static or dynamically activated. Static—constantly visible elements—usually serve design purposes.

Features

The popover feature requires an additional library, "popper.js." There are also different styles available. This is the same as for tooltips.

It can be activated when the page loads with the following code:

```
1   $(function () {
2   $('[data-toggle="popover"]').popover();
3   })
```

For a single item, it looks like this (the selector leads to the button):

```
1    $('#buttonid').popover({});
```

Depending on the content of a button, the application could be critical (see Listing 8-9 and Figure 8-5). Will the effect being bound to button groups (*.btn-group* or *.input-group*), the container element should appear in the <body>. It can otherwise result in side effects (e.g., too broad, loss of rounded corners). It also is not recommended that content overlays be enabled on hidden elements. Bootstrap uses the coordinates of the triggering element for positioning, and without the viewing area this may be inaccurate or invalid. In the deactivated elements you can use content overlays; however, an enclosing container is required (usually a <div>).

If the triggering element is a hyperlink, it can occur on narrow screens. Only then the content of the hyperlink is multiline, and the content superimposition is both horizontal and vertical. This can be inconvenient, because it interferes with the text of the triggering element. With the style white-space: nowrap; on the hyperlink that behavior can be avoided.

The general use as a help text for buttons is as follows:

```
1    <button type="button" class="btn btn-lg btn-danger"
2            data-toggle="popover" title="The Title"
3            data-content="Here is, for example,
         help">Help?</button>
```

Listing 8-9. Popover Place (Popover.html

```
1    <button type="button" class="btn btn-default"
2            data-container="body"
3            data-toggle="popover"
4            data-placement="left"
5            data-content="This is a useful help text.">
6    Placement left
7    </button>
8
```

```
 9   <button type="button" class="btn btn-default"
10           data-container="body"
11           data-toggle="popover"
12           data-placement="top"
13           data-content="This is a useful help text.">
14       Placement above
15   </button>
16
17   <button type="button" class="btn btn-default"
18           data-container="body"
19           data-toggle="popover"
20           data-placement="bottom"
21           data-content="This is a useful help text.">
22       Placement below
23   </button>
24
25   <button type="button" class="btn btn-default"
26           data-container="body"
27           data-toggle="popover"
28           data-placement="right"
29           data-content="This is a useful help text.">
30       Placement right
31   </button>
```

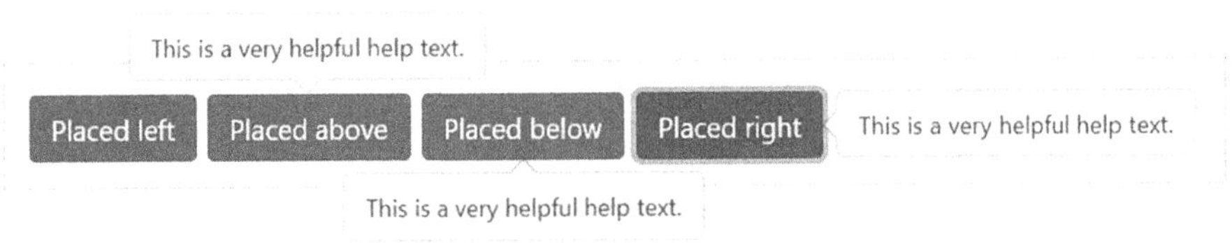

Figure 8-5. Popover placement

Small elements that temporarily appear in the view, such as content overlays, can be easily removed. It is easiest for the user when the next action removes the element. The event "Focus" can accomplish this, because it responds to every other element that gets focus. In addition, the attributes role="button" and tabindex available.

```
1  <a tabindex="0" class="btn btn-lg btn-danger"
2     role="button"
3     data-toggle="popover"
4     data-trigger="focus"
5     title="Help is at hand"
6     data-content="This is the help text!">
7    Can be removed
8  </a>
```

Caution   For this to consistently work, the trigger should be a hyperlink, not a button.

Options

Options may be set as data-attributes in HTML or with code. The suffix of the data-attributes corresponds to the name of the property. Table 8-15 lists the options, Table 8-16 lists the actions, and Table 8-17 lists the events for popovers.

Table 8-15. *Options for Popovers*

Name	Type	Description
animation	Boolean	Animation on appearance
container	String or false	Positioning at another element
delay	Number, object	Delay in milliseconds (Default: 0) can also be an object: { "show": 10, "hide": 10 } then apply for ads and hides different values
html	Boolean	HTML is allowed in the text
content	String	Default content if the element delivers nothing
placement	String, function	"top," "bottom," "left," "right," "auto." With the value "auto" the tooltip is always displayed. When a function is used, the position is determined by this function
selector	String	To select the destination as a selector
template	String	Template in HTML
title	String	Content (text) of tooltips
trigger	String	Trigger: click, hover, focus, manual. Standard: ' "hover focus"
viewport	String, object, function	Standard: { selector: 'body', padding: 0 } or a selector or a selection function

The default template of popover looks like this:

```
1   <div class="popover" role="tooltip">
2     <div class="arrow"></div>
3     <h3 class="popover-title"></h3>
4     <div class="popover-content"></div>
5   </div>
```

The text appears in an element with the class *.popover-content.*

Table 8-16. *Actions for Popovers*

Name	Description
show	Show
hide	Hide
toggle	Switch view state
enable	Enable (default)
disable	Make temporarily not function
dispose	Destroy the element

Table 8-17. *Events for Popovers*

Name	Description
hide.bs.popover	Popover is hiding
show.bs.popover	Popover appears
hidden.bs.popover	Popover was hidden (by animation)
shown.bs.popover	Popover was shown (by animation)
inserted.bs.popover	Return to "show" if the item is placed in the DOM

Message (Alert)

The alerts component produces the same messages to those made with just the class *.alert*.

Features

The additional interaction you get with JavaScript is the ability to hide the element (to close). The message itself also may include other actions. The disable function is created automatically when data-dismiss="alert" is added to the element that triggers the closing process. A "close" button may look like this (within an <div> decorated as alert):

```
1   <button type="button"
2           id="myAlert"
3           class="close"
4           data-dismiss="alert"
5           aria-label="Close">
6     <span aria-hidden="true">&times;</span>
7   </button>
```

Activation is carried out using the method alert():

```
1   $('#myAlert').alert();
```

It may react to closing:

```
1   $('#myAlert').on('closed.bs.alert',
2   function () {
3     // do something...
4   })
```

Options

Options do not exist. The design is accomplished with HTML. Table 8-18 lists the actions and Table 8-19 lists the events for alerts.

Table 8-18. *Action for Alerts*

Name	Description
close	Hide message
dispose	Destroy the component

Table 8-19. *Events for Alerts*

Name	Description
close.bs.popover	Message is closed
closed.bs.popover	Message was closed (after animation)

Action Buttons (Button)

Action buttons respond to states and display them.

Features

With data-toggle="button" you get a button for the user to switch back and forth. It looks like a button, but behaves logically as a checkbox. If this switch is intended to start the page active, it should have the class *.active* and carry the attribute aria-pressed="true."

```
1    <button type="button" class="btn btn-primary"
2    data-toggle="button"
3    aria-pressed="false" autocomplete="off">
4    Simple Switcher
5    </button>
```

By the same token, this also can be used for groups. Here data-toggle="buttons" is used on an element with the class .btn-group. The elements should then be of type checkbox or radio. The design can still be carried out as a button. This behaves as a part of many components and is less technical than using a number of checkboxes or radio buttons.

```
1    <div class="btn-group" data-toggle="buttons">
2      <label class="btn btn-primary active">
3        <input type="checkbox" autocomplete="off" checked> 1
4      </label>
5      <label class="btn btn-primary">
6        <input type="checkbox" autocomplete="off"> 2
7      </label>
8      <label class="btn btn-primary">
9        <input type="checkbox" autocomplete="off"> 3
10     </label>
11   </div>
12   <div class="btn-group" data-toggle="buttons">
13     <label class="btn btn-primary active">
14       <input type="radio" name="options"
15              id="option1" autocomplete="off" checked> 1
16     </label>
17     <label class="btn btn-primary">
18       <input type="radio" name="options"
19              id="option2" autocomplete="off"> 2
20     </label>
```

```
21     <label class="btn btn-primary">
22       <input type="radio" name="options"
23               id="option3" autocomplete="off"> 3
24     </label>
25   </div>
```

Options

Options do not exist. The design is done with HTML. Table 8-20 lists the action for buttons. The only possibility for change via code is to change the text on the button:

```
1    $('#myButton').button('New Text');
```

Table 8-20. *Action for Buttons*

Name	Description
toggle	Toggle the state
dispose	Destroy the component

Content Insertion (Collapse)

Similar content overlay creates the content display (or content suppression, depending on how you look at it). In any case, this element is used to display only temporarily unnecessary content and then releases valuable space again.

Features

What is needed are first-inducing elements, which are either hyperlinks or buttons, as shown in Listing 8-10:

Listing 8-10. Content Insertion (Collapse.html)

```
1    <a class="btn btn-primary"
2    role="button"
3    data-toggle="collapse"
4    href="#collapseExample"
5    aria-expanded="false"
6    aria-controls="collapseExample">
7    Via Link
8    </a>
9    <button class="btn btn-outline-danger"
10     type="button"
11   data-toggle="collapse"
12   data-target="#collapseExample"
13   aria-expanded="false"
14   aria-controls="collapseExample">
15   Via Button
16   </button>
17   <div class="collapse" id="collapseExample">
18   <div class="card card-block card-text">
19          ...
20   </div>
21   </div>
```

The trigger to switch the group is data-toggle="collapse." This either can be a link (with href="#targetId") or a button (with data-target="selector").

The lower portion of the message text is displayed only when one of the buttons has been clicked, as shown in Figure 8-6.

Figure 8-6. *Content is displayed dynamically*

The Aria support is valued internally by the script and should be complemented by matching attributes:

- aria-expanded: indicates which group is open

- aria-controls: indicates which group is controlled by link

- aria-labelledby: indicates which head area refers to the group

Content Groups: The Accordion

The accordion is a frequently used element that offers many design frameworks. Technically, this is a group of navigation elements and dynamic panels that are displayed exclusively in each case.

The individual components have all been introduced. In Bootstrap the accordion is not a stand-alone component, but a combination of basic building blocks.

First, look at the example in Listing 8-11:

Listing 8-11. Content Groups (Accordion.html)

```
1   <div id="accordion" role="tablist" aria-
    multiselectable="true">
2     <div class="card bg-success"
3         role="tab">
4       <h4 class="card-header"
```

```
5                  id="headingOne">
6        <a href="#collapseOne"
7            data-toggle="collapse"
8            data-parent="#accordion"
9            aria-expanded="true"
10           aria-controls="collapseOne">
11         Group 1</a>
12         </h4>
13       <div id="collapseOne"
14           class="collapse in"
15           role="tabpanel"
16            aria-labelledby="headingOne">
17         <div class="card-body card-text">
18           A lot of text in group 1.
19         </div>
20       </div>
21   </div>
22   <div class="card"
23         role="tab">
24     <h4 class="card-header"
25         id="headingTwo">
26       <a href="#collapseTwo"
27           data-toggle="collapse"
28           data-parent="#accordion"
29           aria-expanded="false"
30           aria-controls="collapseTwo">Group 2</a>
31     </h4>
32     <div id="collapseTwo"
33         class="collapse"
34         role="tabpanel"
35         aria-labelledby="headingTwo">
```

```
36        <div class="card-body card-text">
37            A lot of text in group 2.
38        </div>
39      </div>
40    </div>
41    <div class="card"
42          role="tab">
43      <h4 class="card-header"
44          id="headingThree">
45        <a href="#collapseThree"
46            data-toggle="collapse"
47            data-parent="#accordion"
48            aria-expanded="false"
49            aria-controls="collapseThree">
50          Group 3</a>
51      </h4>
52      <div id="collapseThree"
53            class="collapse"
54            role="tabpanel"
55            aria-labelledby="headingThree">
56        <div class="card-block card-text">
57          A lot of text in group 3.
58        </div>
59      </div>
60    </div>
61    </div>
```

The code uses the data-attributes and design of the.*card* class
with related classes. The trigger for the switching of the group is data-
toggle="collapse." This can either be a link (with href="#targetId") or a
button (with data-target="Selector"). When you open a group, the group
that is already open closes automatically, which is data-parent="id" and
uses the ID that refers to the surrounding container element.

The initial state is determined by the class *.in*. Such decorated elements are open on page load, as shown in Figure 8-7.

Figure 8-7. *Contents display*

Activating the code—if data-attributes are not used—is as follows:

```
1   $('.collapse').collapse();
```

Caution   Use either "data-"-attributes or JavaScript. If both are used simultaneously, the script gets confused and the accordion behaves illogically.

Use either "data-"-attributes or JavaScript. If both are used simultaneously, the script gets confused and the accordion behaves illogically.

Options

Options may be set as a "data-"-attributes in HTML or with code.

The suffix of the "data-"-attributes corresponds to the name of the property. Table 8-21 lists the options, Table 8-22 lists the actions, and Table 8-23 lists the events for collapse.

Table 8-21. *Options for Collapse*

Name	Type	Description
parent	String	Selector for the parent element automatic switch
toggle	Boolean	Toggles the collapsible element on invocation

Table 8-22. *Action for Collapse*

Name	Description
show	Show the element
hide	Hide the element
toggle	Switch view state
dispose	Destroy the component

Table 8-23. *Events for Collapse*

Name	Description
hide.bs.collapse	Content is hidden
show.bs.collapse	Content is displayed
hidden.bs.collapse	Contents were hidden (by animation)
shown.bs.collapse	Content has been displayed (after animation)

Image Roundabout (Carousel)

The gyro images (often called carousel) are used to display a picture or content path, which has always just one element that is currently visible.

Features

Listing 8-12 demonstrates an example (see Figure 8-8 for a visual image):

Listing 8-12. Image Roundabout (caroussel.html)

```
1    <div id="carousel-example-generic"
2         class="carousel slide" data-ride="carousel">
3      <ol class="carousel-indicators">
4        <li data-target="#carousel-example-generic"
5            data-slide-to="0" class="active"></li>
6        <li data-target="#carousel-example-generic"
7            data-slide-to="1"></li>
8        <li data-target="#carousel-example-generic"
9            data-slide-to="2"></li>
10     </ol>
11   <div class="carousel-inner" role="listbox">
12       <div class="carousel-item active text-center">
13           <img src="../Res/css3.png" class="d-block w100" />
14       <div class="carousel-caption">
15           CSS 3
16       </div>
17       </div>
18   <div class="carousel-item text-center">
19   <img src="../Res/html5.png" class="d-block w100" />
20   <div class="carousel-caption">
21       HTML 5
22   </div>
23   </div>
24   <div class="carousel-item text-center">
25       <img src="../Res/es6.png" class="d-block w100" />
26   <div class="carousel-caption">
```

```
27        ES 6
28    </div>
29    </div>
30    </div>
31    <a class="left carousel-control"
32        href="#carousel-example-generic"
33        role="button"
34        data-slide="prev">
35    <span class="fa fa-chevron-left"
36        aria-hidden="true"></span>
37    <span class="sr-only">Previous</span>
38    </a>
39    <a class="right carousel-control"
40        href="#carousel-example-generic"
41        role="button"
42        data-slide="next">
43    <span class="fa fa-chevron-right"
44        aria-hidden="true"></span>
45    <span class="sr-only">Next</span>
46    </a>
47    </div>
```

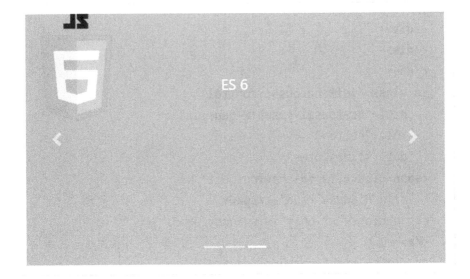

Figure 8-8. *An image of one of the carousel states*

The activation code is as follows:

```
1    $('.carousel').carousel();
```

Caution   This component is not suitable for accessible environments.

Options

Options may be set as a data-attributes in HTML or with code. The suffix of the data-attributes corresponds to the name of the property. Table 8-24 lists the options, Table 8-25 lists the actions, and Table 8-26 lists the events for carousels.

Table 8-24. *Options for Carousel*

Name	Type	Description
interval	Number	Time until the next element, default is 5,000 ms
pause	String	Stops the indexing, as long as the mouse is over the element
wrap	Boolean	Continuous indexing or stepwise
keyboard	Boolean	Responds to the keyboard
ride	string	Autoplay
touch	Boolean	Activate touch support

Table 8-25. *Actions for Carousel*

Name	Description
cycle	Change to the next item
pause	Stop
prev	Previous entry
next	Next entry
dispose	Destroy the component

Table 8-26. *Events for Carousel*

Name	Description
slide.bs.carousel	Start a movement
slid.bs.carousel	End a movement

Summary

In this chapter you learned the JavaScript-API and how to get additional functionality through programming the components with just a few lines of code. Some components do not function without JavaScript properly. This is why it's important to have the API handy even if there is no need to change the default behavior.

APPENDIX

A Gentle Introduction to Sass

Sass (syntactically awesome style sheets) is an extension to CSS and adds interactivity and features such as variables, formulas, and functions. For Bootstrap developers it's a big deal to work with it, as Bootstrap 4.x was entirely written in Sass. This appendix provides an introduction to the important parts of the Sass language. Please refer to the official documentation[1] for further details.

How It Works

Sass is a language that compiles down to static CSS. That makes it possible to greatly enhance the features of CSS, but it requires an additional build step before you can send it to a browser. Most modern development environments have ready-to-use compilers, and there is almost no effort to get Sass into real projects.

In Bootstrap it makes sense to work with Sass to change parts of the default settings, add private modifications, or just have a more robust style environment. Designing styles in Sass from the beginning can save a lot of time.

---

[1]Sass, `https://sass-lang.com`.

© Jörg Krause 2020
J. Krause, *Introducing Bootstrap 4*, https://doi.org/10.1007/978-1-4842-6203-0

However, understanding the basic behavior is necessary to avoid problems. The main issue is that replacing dynamic parts with static ones means essentially creating a series of copies. If your Sass function accepts ten different values as parameters, the compiler will create ten static blocks of CSS code with the parameters applied. Smaller Sass code blocks may grow dramatically due to this behavior. Designing clever Sass is essential to get clean, understandable CSS afterwards. On the other hand, some parts such as variables may not create so much code, and can still provide dramatic benefits. In general, just check the created code and assure that it is not suffering from code obesity.

Sass comes in two basic coding styles (and corresponding file extensions): Sass and Scss. Despite the obvious name of *.sass*, the style called Scss (*.scss*) is more common and the one used in this chapter. It's also the one used in Bootstrap. Sass style is more compact, avoiding curly braces and semicolons. But it is not compatible with CSS. That means you cannot paste pure CSS in a Sass file without transforming it first. You can find many examples for proper styling on the Web, and most of this is pure CSS. So copying rule sets into your project without thinking about different syntax is essential. Here the Scss coding style of Sass comes into play. It's completely backward compatible—or in other words, valid CSS is always valid Scss.

First Steps

Static rules in CSS are the biggest drawback. Imagine that you colorize dozens of styles for headings with *blue*. Imagine you have also used the very color for some horizontal rules. Now someone (usually, your customer) decides that the headers need an adjustment and that a better color would be *azure*. But the rules remain. So you cannot use search and replace as a strategy; instead, it is manual work. It's boring, error-prone, and essentially nonsense, because at exactly the moment you're finished, another decision comes along the way.

To start without a project, I recommend using the web site `https://www.sassmeister.com/`. Enter some Sass and get the resulting CSS immediately.

Using Sass in Applications

Whether you want to use Sass in conjunction with Bootstrap, modifying the styles or applying templates, or just use Sass as a modern way to create CSS, a few preparation steps are necessary.

Sass requires a pre-processor that converts the scss-files into regular CSS a browser can read. Which tool exactly fulfills your needs depends on the development workflow. For beginners there are two possible ways. First, you compile Sass directly using the Sass toolset. That's the best option if you have no workflow yet and need to see results immediately. Second, add a hook into your preferred build tool. As an example, I'm going to use Webpack here and show how to add Sass to the build process.

The Sass Toolset

Web projects are usually built on top of NodeJs. This includes the usage of a *project.json* file to organize a project. You can find a ready-to-use project in the Github project that accompanies this book.

- `https://github.com/joergkrause/bootstrap4-book`

The examples in this appendix are all in the subfolder *src/sass*. In the *package.json* I've installed the Sass tool causing this command:

```
1   $ npm i sass -D
```

This downloads the compiler and includes the reference in the project file:

```
1    "devDependencies": {
2       "sass": "^1.26.9"
3    }
```

Now, you can execute this command locally. That means the *node_modules/.bin/* folder contains a command line interface (CLI) that calls the compiler. This folder is connected to the "scripts" section in the *package.json* file. The scripts execute with npm run <script>. The script section in the sample project actually looks like this:

```
1    "scripts": {
2       "sass": "sass"
3    }
```

That may look a bit strange, but the reason is that the left "sass" is the name to run, while the right one is the actual tool. If it's being named that way, the path to the *.bin* folder resolves automatically. It's just convenient to use it like this.

The Sass compiler has several options. Refer to the manual to learn all of them. The usage looks like this (for a single file):

```
1    $ sass <input.scss> [output.css]
2    $ sass <input.scss>:<output.css> <target-dir>
```

In case of the npm scenario the call looks similar:

```
1    $ npm run sass <input.scss> [output.css]
```

Usually a single file is fine, because Sass has a module concept and you can reference more files from a scss-file. In case of a multifile scenario there are more options. A few options can be added using command line switches:

- --watch: watch style sheets and re-compile after a change happens.

- --style=compressed: reduce file size of compiled CSS.

- --no-source-map: suppress the debugger support (source map).

The default behavior is an expanded, human-readable output. Compression is often part of a bigger workflow that includes JavaScript and HTML. Especially for learning, I'd recommend not using the compression algorithm.

The source map is also always available. This is a file that matches the Sass portions to its CSS counterparts. If you now open the CSS in a browser and use the developer tools (F12), the browser tries to read the generated *.map-file. That way you can see and edit the scss material directly without "re-thinking" it in CSS.

Now, if you want to compile one of the examples, just enter this:

```
1    $ npm run sass ./src/sass/variables.scss:./dist/css/
variable.css
```

Here, I'm using the source folder src, the path to the examples, sass, and a distinct scss-file. Then the source file is pulled, followed by the output file. The last parameter is the destination folder, usually called dist (for distribution).

Using NodeJs

However, the options are somehow limited. So, let's extend the environment a little bit and add another tool, named node-sass. It's not really another one, it's just a binding for Sass with a few more path and file options that match better with the typical ways in web projects.

```
1   $ npm i node-sass -D
```

We could change the script's name or add another one. A much better way is to use the capabilities of NodeJs to write JavaScript programs. The one shown next (Listing A-1) converts all *scss*-files in one single step:

Listing A-1. Calling the Sass Compiler in NodeJs

```
1    const sass = require('node-sass');
2    const fs = require('fs');
3    const path = require('path');
4
5    function compileSass(file) {
6      console.log('Converting file ', file)
7      sass.render({
8        file: `./src/sass/${file}.scss`,
9        sourceMap: true,
10       outFile: `./dist/css/${file}.css`
11     }, function (err, result) {
12       if (err) {
13         console.error(err);
14       }
15       if (!err) {
16         // No errors during the compilation, write this
                  result on the disk
17         fs.writeFile(`./dist/css/${file}.css`, result.css,
              function (err) {
```

```
18          if (!err) {
19            console.log('Done css');
20          }
21        });
22        fs.writeFile(`./dist/css/${file}.css.map`,
23                    result.map, (err) => {
24          if (!err) {
25            console.log('Done map');
26          }
27        });
28      }
29
30    });
31  }
32
33  fs.readdir('./src/sass', (err, files) => {
34    files
35      .filter(f => /\.scss$/.test(f))
36      .forEach(file => compileSass(path.basename
        (file, '.scss')));
37  });
```

You'll find it for immediate execution in the path *./tools/sass.js*.
Execute it using the NodeJs command line:

```
1   $ node ./tools/sass.js
```

It is also added to the *package.json* for an even more convenient call
(excerpt from *package.json*):

```
1   "scripts": {
2     "sass": "sass",
3     "ns": "node ./tools/sass.js"
4   },
```

Now, the following command converts all your sass files:

```
1    $ npm run ns
```

Using WebPack

WebPack is by far the most common tool to build web applications. It's highly extensible by plug-ins that exist for almost all tasks. For Sass there are several ways of integration. The following example shows a simple integration for common tasks.

First, install WebPack locally. The following command includes the CLI (command line interface):

```
1    $ npm i webpack webpack-cli -D
```

Next, configuration is required. An example for just one task—compiling Sass—is included in the example project named *webpack. config.js*. To add the plug-ins you'll need this command:

```
1    $ npm i sass-loader style-loader css-loader mini-css-
     extract-plugin -D
```

This also requires node-sass; you can skip it if it was installed in the previous step.

More details can be found here: `https://webpack.js.org/ loaders/sass-loader/`.

WebPack is primarily a JavaScript builder. It's not designed to simply compile. But the results are astonishing if you follow the path. The following file (Listing A-2) is a minimal WebPack configuration.

Listing A-2. WebPack Configuration

```
1    const { join } = require('path');
2
3    module.exports = {
4      entry: './src/sass/main.js',
```

```
 5     mode: 'development',
 6     output: {
 7       path: join(__dirname, './dist'),
 8       filename: 'bundle.js'
 9     },
10     module: {
11       rules: [
12         {
13           test: /\.s(a|c)ss$/,
14           loader: [
15             'style-loader',
16             'css-loader',
17             {
18               loader: 'sass-loader',
19               options: {
20                 sourceMap: true
21               }
22             }
23           ]
24         }
25       ]
26     },
27     resolve: {
28       extensions: ['.scss']
29     }
30   }
```

This makes WebPack to read a JavaScript file, *main.js*, executing and processing it using the provided rules. Then it outputs a single file, *bundle. js*. Just add it to your *index.html* and all styles magically appear. The main. js, however, is extremely simple:

```
1    import './variables.scss';
```

It is this single line with the *scss*-file as an import. Add more if you need multiple files. A typical *html*-file could look like Listing A-3:

Listing A-3. Html File

```
1    <!DOCTYPE html>
2    <html lang="en">
3    <head>
4      <meta charset="UTF-8">
5      <meta name="viewport" content="width=device-width,
         initial-scale=1.0">
6      <title>Document</title>
7    </head>
8    <body>
9      <h1>Test</h1>
10
11     <script src="bundle.js"></script>
12   </body>
13   </html>
```

Two things are achieved here. First, the compilation of JavaScript, TypeScript, or other parts now includes the compilation of Sass. Second, regardless of the number of imports, the result is just one file, pure JavaScript, and no additional <link> elements are needed to load CSS.

The loaders are responsible for all the magic. Here we use these three:

- 'style-loader': creates `style` nodes from JS strings.

- 'css-loader': translates CSS into CommonJS.

- 'sass-loader': compiles Sass to CSS.

The overhead for the JavaScript based loader is roughly 8KB, which makes sense if you have at least 10 KB of CSS code to distribute. In real-life projects this is almost always the case. You can execute the WebPack command by simply typing "Webpack."

Now it's time to learn about Sass itself.

Interactive Sass

Here Sass will provide the first great feature: variables.

Variables

Imagine the example shown in Listing A-4:

Listing A-4. Define Variables (variables.scss)

```
1   $myfont:  Helvetica, sans-serif;
2   $hrcolor: blue;
3   $hxcolor: #8888FF;
4
5   h1 {
6     font: 100% $myfont;
7     color: $hxcolor;
8   }
9   hr {
10    color: $hrcolor;
11  }
```

Here you can simply change the color for the variable and it will replace only the parts where the variable appears. The variables do not have types. It's not really like a programming language, even if there are some operators. Sass detects the type if necessary, but you don't need to worry about this too much. For most values it's a pure copy operation, with the variable being replaced by its value.

Dealing with Defaults

Consider importing data from Bootstrap. You want to overwrite values to customize Bootstrap. This is pretty simple if you use the Sass variables *before* the actual import. Compared with a programming language this sounds odd, but it's exactly the way defaults work in Sass.

See the following excerpt from Bootstrap's Sass definition:

Listing A-5. Bootstrap's Variables Defined in Sass (Excerpt)

```
1    $gray-base:          #000 !default;
2    $gray-darker:        lighten($gray-base, 13.5%)
                          !default; // #222
3    $gray-dark:          lighten($gray-base, 20%)
                          !default;   // #333
4    $gray:               lighten($gray-base, 33.5%)
                          !default; // #555
5    $gray-light:         lighten($gray-base, 46.7%)
                          !default; // #777
6    $gray-lighter:       lighten($gray-base, 93.5%)
                          !default; // #eee
7
8    $brand-primary:      darken(#428bca, 6.5%) !default;
                          // #337ab7
9    $brand-success:      #5cb85c !default;
10   $brand-info:         #5bc0de !default;
11   $brand-warning:      #f0ad4e !default;
12   $brand-danger:       #d9534f !default;
13
```

```
14   //== Scaffolding
15   //
16   //## Settings for some of the most global styles.
17
18   //** Background color for `<body>`.
19   $body-bg:              #fff !default;
20   //** Global text color on `<body>`.
21   $text-color:           $gray-dark !default;
22
23   //** Global textual link color.
24   $link-color:           $brand-primary !default;
25   //** Link hover color set via `darken()` function.
26   $link-hover-color:     darken($link-color, 15%) !default;
27   //** Link hover decoration.
28   $link-hover-decoration: underline !default;
```

All the variables are decorated with the !default switch. That means literally: "I'm a default value, if the very same name is already in use, then silently skip me." That's the reason why you have to define the replacement *before* the imported definition. As soon as you know the variable used in Bootstrap, you can easily customize it without changing anything in the original files. Consider this example:

```
1   $primary: purple;
2   $danger: red;
3   @import "../../node_modules/bootstrap/scss/bootstrap.scss";
```

Here the colors of the primary and danger semantics are changed. Because many colors derive from this global definition, all these children will change, too. For instance, this includes shadows and borders that follow the main color definitions.

Using WebPack   If you use WebPack, you can shorten the import like this:

```
@import "~bootstrap"
```

WebPack is smart enough to recognize the module definition in the package and load the right part. The leading "~" sign (tilde) is a shortcut for *node_modules*.

Nesting Styles

CSS is great for addressing elements depending on their appearance in the document object model. Often the hierarchy is essential. In CSS you express this by operators, such as ">," " ," "," "," , and so on. That's powerful, but hard to read and far from being intuitive. In Sass you can write it as a hierarchy in a much more natural way, as in Listing A-6:

Listing A-6. Define Variables (nested.scss)

```
1    nav {
2      ul {
3        margin: 0;
4        padding: 0;
5        list-style: none;
6      }
7
8      li { display: inline-block; }
9
10     a {
11       display: block;
12       padding: 6px 12px;
```

```
13        text-decoration: none;
14    }
15  }
```

Operators

The operators are similar to other programming languages, with one major exception. They are not entirely numeric, but also incorporate the units. See the following example in Listing A-7:

Listing A-7. Using Operators (ops.scss)

```
1   .container {
2     width: 100%;
3   }
4
5   article[role="main"] {
6     float: left;
7     width: 600px / 960px * 100%;
8   }
9
10  aside[role="complementary"] {
11    float: right;
12    width: 300px / 960px * 100%;
13  }
```

As you can see, the units are still beneath their values and part of the formula. That's even more astonishing: that a mixup is possible, adding or multiplying different units. Imagine this simple definition:

```
1   $size: 100px + 1mm;
2
3   div {
```

```
4    width: $size;
5  }
```

Now, the CSS looks like this:

```
1  div {
2    width: 103.7795275591px;
3  }
```

Though adding the units "px" and "mm" is neither obvious nor easy, Sass makes it as simple as possible. However, sometimes it's harder to get. See this expression:

```
1  $size: 10px * 10px;
```

It's not assignable, because it's *10px*px* (called "square pixels," only useful for further operations). The correct formula would be like this:

```
1  $size: 10px * 10;
```

This would be "100px," indeed.

The list of operators is huge and on par with common programming languages.

Interpolation

A lot of places allow the usage of variables without additional string operators. This is called interpolation. See the following example in Listing A-8:

Listing A-8. Mixin with Interpolation

```
1  @mixin some-text($name, $top-or-bottom, $left-or-right) {
2    .text-#{$name} {
3      background-image: url("/images/#{$name}.png");
```

```
4        position: absolute;
5        #{$top-or-bottom}: 0;
6        #{$left-or-right}: 0;
7      }
8    }
```

The trick is using the #{variable-name} syntax. It's not limited to values; even names and rules support such a replacement:

- Selectors in style rules

- Property names in declarations

- Custom property values

- CSS at-rules, @extends and plain CSS imports (with @import)

- Quoted or unquoted strings at any place

- Special functions

- Plain CSS function names

Functions

Sass comes with several functions to handle values. There are several modules that provide functions:

- Color: handle color changes.

- List: create list of values for iterations (such as an array).

- Map: create list of key-value pairs for iterations (such as a dictionary).

- Math: mathematical function beyond the scope of operators.

- Meta: helpers; such as load CSS and include, call functions, and check features.

- Selector: helpers for dealing with CSS selectors.

- String: typical string functions such as "index," "insert," and "length."

It is beyond the scope of this book to cover all of them. To give you an idea of the power, see the common usage of color functions in Bootstrap, namely darken and lighten.

```
1   $table-dark-bg:            $gray-800 !default;
2   $table-dark-border-color:  lighten($table-dark-bg, 7.5%)
                               !default;

3
4   $dropdown-link-color:      $gray-900 !default;
5   $dropdown-link-hover-color: darken($gray-900, 5%) !default;
```

Here, a base color is taken and made a little darker or lighter. That's much easier than calculating the colors using some sort of photo software.

Modularization

Splitting large files into parts is always a good idea. There are several ways to structure the code better than using pure CSS.

Partials

Partials are what modules mean in JavaScript. Instead of having huge files with thousands of lines, it's much better to have several smaller files. A partial is defined by using an underscore as the first character of the file name. It's primarily an instruction to the compiler to not create another CSS, but to let it alone until it's requested by some code. The request uses a special function like this:

```
1    @use partial
```

As you can see, the *@use* command doesn't require the underscore, nor does it require the file extensions. If your file is named "_partial.scss," it's just fine.

Some predefined modules can be imported by this command as well.

Mixins

Functions or methods in other languages are called mixins. It makes sense to have a different name here because the result is not a function call but a number of copies, depending on the parameters. See Listing A-9 for a usage example:

Listing A-9. Mixins and Includes (mixin.scss)

```
1    @mixin no-list {
2      margin: 0;
3      padding: 0;
4      list-style: none;
5    }
6
7    @mixin simple-list {
8      @include no-list;
```

```
 9
10    li {
11      display: inline-block;
12      margin: {
13        left: -2px;
14        right: 2em;
15      }
16    }
17   }
18
19   nav ul {
20     @include simple-list;
21   }
```

This example does not use parameters, so the resulting CSS is easy.

```
 1   nav ul {
 2     margin: 0;
 3     padding: 0;
 4     list-style: none;
 5   }
 6   nav ul li {
 7     display: inline-block;
 8     margin-left: -2px;
 9     margin-right: 2em;
10   }
```

The Sass compiler is smart enough to avoid duplications, if the addressing model of CSS allows this using distinct rules. But that's not always the case. Be careful using mixins and check the compiled code. See Listing A-10 for a mixin with parameters:

Listing A-10. Mixin with Parameters (mixinparam.scss)

```
1    @mixin replace-text($image, $x: 50%, $y: 50%) {
2      text-indent: -99999em;
3      overflow: hidden;
4      text-align: left;
5
6      background: {
7        image: $image;
8        repeat: no-repeat;
9        position: $x $y;
10      }
11    }
12
13    .mail-icon {
14      @include replace-text(url("/images/mail.svg"), 0);
15    }
16    .inbox-icon {
17      @include replace-text(url("/images/inbox.svg"), 0);
18    }
```

While this looks easy to use, the resulting CSS is quite verbose:

```
1    .mail-icon {
2      text-indent: -99999em;
3      overflow: hidden;
4      text-align: left;
5      background-image: url("/images/mail.svg");
6      background-repeat: no-repeat;
7      background-position: 0 50%;
8    }
9
```

```
10    .inbox-icon {
11      text-indent: -99999em;
12      overflow: hidden;
13      text-align: left;
14      background-image: url("/images/inbox.svg");
15      background-repeat: no-repeat;
16      background-position: 0 50%;
17    }
```

As you can see, it's just the content of the mixin duplicated with the parameters set properly. If there are hundreds of different mixins-calls in your code, this would blow up the CSS file.

Conditions

To make mixins even more powerful, they can contain @if instructions like this (see Listing A-11):

Listing A-11. Mixin with a Conditional Part

```
1     :
2     @mixin image($size, $radius: 0) {
3       width: $size;
4       height: $size;
5
6       @if $radius != 0 {
7         border-radius: $radius;
8       }
9     }
10
11    .icon {
12      @include image(32px, $radius: 2px);
13    }
```

For a radius of 0 the *border-radius* rule doesn't make sense, so it's being excluded in such a call.

Loops

In a similar way, you can use @for to create loops. See Listing A-12 for an example:

Listing A-12. Mixin with Loops (mixinloop.scss)

```
1   @mixin order($height, $selectors...) {
2     @for $i from 0 to length($selectors) {
3       #{nth($selectors, $i + 1)} {
4         position: absolute;
5         height: $height;
6         margin-top: $i * $height;
7       }
8     }
9   }
10
11  @include order(150px, "input[name='name']",
       "input[name='address']");
```

Here again, the risk is creating many duplicates even more easily.

Summary

This appendix gave a short introduction into the main features of Sass, its usage in Bootstrap, and how to get a Sass compiler up and running.

Index

A

Accessible Rich Internet
  Applications
  Suite (ARIA), 9, 11, 162
Active components
  action buttons
    features, 313, 314
    options, 315
  content insertion/collapse
    accordion, 317
    actions, 321
    aria support, 317
    Collapse.html, 315, 316
    content groups, 317–319
    data-attributes, 320
    display, 316, 317, 320
    events, 321
    options, 321
  content overlay/popover
    actions, 311
    container element, 307
    events, 311
    help text, 307
    options, 310
    placement, 307, 308
    popper.js., 306
    tabindex, 309

    template, 311
    triggering element, 307
  drop-down menu
    actions, 292, 293
    behavior, 291
    callback function, 294
    events, 293
    HTML, 293
    hyperlinks, 294
    options, 292
  image roundabout/carousel
    actions, 325
    events, 325
    features, 322, 323
    options, 325
  messages
    actions, 313
    events, 313
    features, 312
  modal dialogs, 277
    (see Modal dialogs)
  reversible tabulators
    actions, 300
    events, 301
    features, 298–300
  scroll bar supervisor/scrollspy
    actions, 297
    events, 297

© Jörg Krause 2020
J. Krause, *Introducing Bootstrap 4*, https://doi.org/10.1007/978-1-4842-6203-0

T, U, V

W, X, Y, Z

Printed in the United States
By Bookmasters